D0079609

WOMEN BEYOND FREUD

New Concepts of Feminine Psychology

WOMEN BEYOND FREUD

New Concepts of Feminine Psychology

Edited by

MILTON M. BERGER, M.D.

with chapters by

MARIANNE HORNEY ECKARDT • CAROL GILLIGAN
DOUGLAS H. INGRAM • HELEN SINGER KAPLAN
HAROLD I. LIEF • JEAN BAKER MILLER
SILVIA W. OLARTE • SUSAN QUINN • MARIO RENDON

BRUNNER/MAZEL *Publishers* • NEW YORK

Poetry excerpts on pp. 122 & 123 are from: Graham, Jorie; "The Age of Reason," in *Erosion*. Copyright © 1983 by Princeton University Press. Reprinted by permisson of Princeton University Press.

Library of Congress Cataloging-in-Publication Data

Women beyond Freud : new concepts of feminine psychology / edited by Milton M. Berger ; with chapters by Marianne Horney Eckardt ... [et al.].

p. cm.

Includes bibliographical references.

ISBN 0-87630-709-8

1. Women—Psychology—Congresses. 2. Horney, Karen, 1885-1952—Congresses. I. Berger, Milton Miles.

HQ1206.W8744 ~~1993~~ 1994

155.3'33 dc20 93-8820

CIP

Published by

BRUNNER/MAZEL, INC.

19 Union Square West

New York, NY 10003

Manufactured in the United States of America

10 9 8 7 6 5 4 3 2 1

CONTENTS

ABOUT THE CONTRIBUTORS

Milton M. Berger, M.D. President, Association for the Advancement of Psychoanalysis; Clinical Professor of Psychiatry, New York University School of Medicine; Fellow, American Academy of Psychoanalysis, American Psychiatric Association, American Group Psychotherapy Association. Author of *Working with People Called Patients*, New York: Brunner/Mazel, 1978.

Marianne Horney Eckardt, M.D. Former President, American Academy of Psychoanalysis; formerly Clinical Associate Professor of Psychiatry, New York Medical College.

Carol Gilligan, Ph.D. Professor, Human Development and Psychology, Graduate School of Education, Harvard University, and a founding member of the Harvard Project on Women's Psychology and Girl's Development. Author, *In a Different Voice: Psychological Theory and Women's Development*, Cambridge: Harvard University Press, 1982.

Douglas H. Ingram, M.D. Clinical Associate Professor of Psychiatry, New York Medical College; Faculty member, Training and Supervising Analyst, American Institute for Psychoanalysis and also at the Psychoanalytic Institute of Dept. of Psychiatry and Behavioral Sciences, New York Medical College; editor of the *American Journal of Psychoanalysis;* Editor, *Final Lectures of Dr. Karen Horney*, New York: Norton, 1987.

Helen Singer Kaplan, M.D., Ph.D. Clinical Professor of Psychiatry, Cornell University Medical College; Founder and Director of Human Sexuality Program, Payne Whitney Clinic, The New York Hospital/Cornell Medical Center; Fellow, American Academy of Psychoanalysis and American Psychiatric Association. Author of many books on human sexuality including *The New Sex Therapy*, (1974), *Disorders of Sexual Desire*, (1979), *Sexual Aversion, Sexual*

Phobia, and Panic Disorder, (1987), and *The New Injection Treatment for Impotence*, (1993), New York: Brunner/Mazel.

Harold I. Lief, M.D. Professor Emeritus of Psychiatry, University of Pennsylvania School of Medicine; Psychiatrist Emeritus, Pennsylvania Hospital; pioneer in sex therapy; former President, American Academy of Psychoanalysis; Charter Fellow, American College of Psychoanalysts; Life Fellow, American Psychiatric Association.

Jean Baker Miller, M.D. Clinical Professor of Psychiatry, Boston University School of Medicine; Director of Education, Stone Center for Developmental Services and Studies; Fellow, American Academy of Psychoanalysis and American Psychiatric Association; Author of *Psychoanalysis and Women*, New York: Brunner/Mazel, 1973, and *Toward a New Psychology of Women*, Boston: Beacon Press, 1976.

Silvia Olarte, M.D. Clinical Associate Professor of Psychiatry, New York Medical College; Supervisor and Training Analyst, Psychoanalytic Institute, New York Medical College; Fellow, American Academy of Psychoanalysis.

Susan Quinn, Author of *A Mind of Her Own: The Life of Karen Horney*, New York: Summit Books, 1978.

Mario Rendon, M.D. Director of Psychiatry, Lincoln Medical and Mental Health Center, New York; Professor of Clinical Psychiatry, New York Medical College; Training and Supervising Analyst, American Institute for Psychoanalysis; former Editor, *American Journal of Psychoanalysis.*

INTRODUCTION

MILTON M. BERGER, M. D.

The origins of *Women Beyond Freud: New Concepts of Feminine Psychology* can be found in an all-day conference, which took place on November 2, 1991, in New York City to celebrate the 50th anniversary of the founding of the Karen Horney Psychoanalytic Center in New York City in 1941. This volume contains some of the best papers and commentaries of this historic meeting, which was attended by over 2,000 mental health professionals and the general public. It will serve as an enduring testament to the seminal contributions made by Karen Horney, who is called by Janet Sayers (1991) one of the four "mothers of psychoanalysis" in her recent book of the same name.

Karen Horney, who was my teacher and faculty advisor 45 years ago at the American Institute for Psychoanalysis, where she was dean from 1941 until her death on December 4, 1952, was the first woman member of the Berlin Psychoanalytic Institute and Center. Along with Helene Deutsch, Anna Freud, and Melanie Klein (the other mothers of psychoanalysis), she dared to question the male-centered theories and clinical practices of Sigmund Freud. These four women paid more attention than Freud to understanding the influence of mothering and other interpersonal processes in the development and shaping of individual personality and character structure. Horney concentrated on the importance of family and societal cultures in molding the destiny of individuals and went far beyond Freud's insistent focus on "anatomy as destiny." She detailed in many early and later writings the powerful impact of unclear, subtle messages and forces in clearly shaping our lives.

The major contributions made by Horney on "feminine psychology" were collected, translated, and published by Drs. Harold

Kelman, Edward R. Clemmons, John M. Meth, Edward Schattner, and Gerda F. Willner (1967), who served as a committee for The Association for Advancement of Psychoanalysis (also founded by Horney in 1941) to fulfill that task. This collection of 14 papers pertaining to feminine psychology were written in German between 1922 and 1937; since these papers have been available in English they have been hailed by the feminist movement, which, as Marianne Horney Eckardt so aptly states, "recognized in her an early champion of their cause" (this volume). There is no doubt that the appeal of these early papers, which contain views so radically different from Freud's disparaging position on women, contributed to the large attendance at the anniversary meeting.

The titles of these aforementioned papers will surely give the reader an awareness of the broad scope of Horney's interests as she repeatedly protested the views of Freud and his most orthodox followers. "On the Genesis of the Castration Complex in Women" was delivered in Berlin in 1921 (Vol. 5, pp. 50–65). Her next paper on "The Flight from Womanhood: The Masculinity-Complex in Women as Viewed by Men and Women" (1926) was published in the *International Journal of Psycho-analysis* (Vol. 3, pp. 324–339). Significant new themes espoused by Horney in this important paper are that female and male biology are different but equal and that female biology is not inferior to male biology. In this paper Horney also focuses on motherhood: "the blissful consciousness of bearing a new life within oneself . . . the ineffable happiness of the increasing expectation of the appearance of the new being . . . the joy when it finally makes its appearance and one holds it for the first time in one's arms . . . the deep pleasurable feeling of satisfaction in suckling it and the happiness of the whole period when the infant needs her care . . . from the biological point of view woman has in motherhood, or in the capacity for motherhood, a quite indisputable and by no means negligible physiological superiority."

We can clearly see with what spunk and personal intensity Horney takes on the struggle against Freud's theories regarding women and against the writings of George Simmel, the social philosopher who saw our whole civilization as a masculine one. The fact that Simmel and others went along with the idea that it is quite right for the standards of state, law, morality, religion, and science to be created by men; for the standards that mankind has used to estimate the value of male and female nature to be masculine standards; for the concept of a human being to be equated with the concept of man. All these facts of her times led Horney to feel affirmed in her beliefs that women were not being seen in their own right and that she must do something to change the status quo. And she did!

Earlier in her professional career Horney had written,

> My scientific interest concentrated more and more on female psychology and connected fields such as the differentiation between masculine and feminine psychology, general disturbances in relation between the two sexes and marriage problems. As psychology has been until now mostly worked at from the side of men, it seems to me to be the given task for a woman psychologist, or at least I think it to be mine, to work out a fuller understanding for specifically female trends and attitudes in life. (Quinn, 1978)

The next article in the collection on *Feminine Psychology* is a brief contribution entitled, "Inhibited Femininity: A Psychological Contribution to the Problem of Frigidity" (1926–1927), which was published in *Zeitschrift f. Sexualwissenschaft* (Vol. 13, pp. 67–77). Horney masterfully examines overt and covert life experiences that become endogenous and exogenous factors, which she believed are different in each individual case of inhibited femininity, and offers many clues as to what needs to be reviewed and analyzed in the attempt to undermine blockages to sexual fulfillment.

The importance and timeliness of the contributions made by Horney are again evident in her paper on "The Problem of the Monogamous Ideal" read at the Tenth International Psychoanalytical Congress in Innsbruch, September 3, 1927. It was published in the *International Journal of Psycho-analysis* (Vol. 4, pp. 318–331, 1928). Here she took on a subject that occupies us very much today when so few first marriages last, namely, the subject of monogamy in marriage and the matrimonial conflicts caused by the demand for monogamy, which is so often not lived up to. Horney, while expanding our ideas on matrimonial conflicts, offers no easy solution. In

1931 she published a paper on "Premenstrual Tension" in the *Zeitschrift f. Psychoanalytische Padagogek* (Vol. 5, No. 5/6, pp. 1–7) in which she talks of therapeutically influencing the many psychological and functionally induced disorders of menstruation and pays special attention to those disorders occurring in the days before the onset of menstrual flow. Again we witness her timeliness in touching on what we now label diagnostically as PMS (premenstrual syndrome). Without today's knowledge of hormonal changes and treatments, Horney focused in this paper on such causes for premenstrual tension as the issue of a stronger libidinal drive, issues related to wishes to bear or not to bear a child, and that the onset of menstrual bleeding is so often accompanied not only by a sense of physical relief, but also relief from the conflicts associated with fantasies of pregnancy.

The up-to-date pertinence of Horney's thinking is found in "The Distrust Between Sexes," which she read before the Berlin-Brandenburg Branch of the German Women's Medical Association on November 20, 1930, and published in *Die Arztin* (Vol. 7, pp. 5–12, 1931):

> Woman is said to be deeply rooted in the personal and emotional spheres, which is wonderful; but unfortunately, this makes her incapable of exercising justice and objectivity, thereby disqualifying her for positions in law and government and in the spiritual community. She is said to be at home only in the realm of eros. Spiritual matters are alien to her innermost being, and she is at odds with cultural trends. She therefore is, as Asians frankly state, a second-rate being. Woman may be industrious and useful but is, alas, incapable of productive and independent work. She is, indeed, prevented from real accomplishment by the deplorable, bloody tragedies of menstruation and childbirth. And so every man silently thanks his God, just as the pious Jew does in his prayers, that he was not created a woman.

We see here her capacity for sarcasm and forthrightness, which was to fuel her future work as she continued to take on the authorities whose word was considered to be "the law."

She tackled the "Problems of Marriage" in the seventh of her papers on feminine psychology published as "Zur Problematik der Ehe" in *Psychoanalytische Bewegung* (Vol. 4, pp. 212–223, 1932). She asked important questions such as,

> Why are good marriages so rare? marriages that do not stifle the developmental potential of the partners, marriages in which undercurrents of tension do not reverberate in the home or in which they are so intense they have brought about a benevolent indifference? Could it be that the institution of marriage cannot be reconciled with certain facts of human existence? Is marriage perhaps only an illusion about to disappear, or is modern man particularly incapable of giving it substance? Are we admitting to its failure or to our own when we condemn it? Why is marriage so often the death of love? must we succumb to this situation as if it were an unavoidable law, or are we subject to forces within us, variable in content and impact, and perhaps recognizable and even avoidable, yet playing havoc with us?

In this important paper Horney emphasizes the necessity for "an inner renunciation of claims on the partner . . . I mean claims in the sense of demands and not wishes."

In her last book, *Neurosis and Human Growth* (1950), Horney spelled out in great detail the devastation to self and others, which stem from making neurotic expectations on others in situations where we have a right to hope but not expect. The unfulfilled expectations cause such anger that relationships become corroded to the "point of no return!"

I hope these excerpts from her papers from 1922 through 1932 will spark you to review the last chapters in her book of collected papers entitled, "The Dread of Woman!" (1932), "The Denial of the Vagina" (1933), "Psychogenic Factors in Functional Female Disorders" (1933), "Maternal Conflicts" (1933), "The Overvaluation of Love" (1934), "The Problem of Feminine Masochism" (1935), "Personality Changes in Female Adolescents" (1935) and "The Neurotic Need for Love" (1937).

Horney's papers on feminine psychology represented the first major differences with the "master" on this major subject of psychoanalysis by an accepted member of the Freudian International Psychoanalytic Society. They also served to broaden and strengthen Horney's beliefs in the importance of culture on the shaping of each person, male as well as female. This was a stepping stone in the working through of her evolving ideas on what influences and molds in myriads of unseen ways the development of each and every human being. While searching and researching her own inner self as well as her patients, Horney more clearly formulated and organized her theory, which led to the publication of a series of works published in many languages starting with *The Neurotic Personality of Our Time* in 1937. This was followed by *New Ways in Psychoanalysis* (1939), *Self-Analysis* (1942b), *Our Inner Conflicts* (1945), *Are You Considering Psychoanalysis?* (1946), and then what was to be her last book, *Neurosis and Human Growth* (1950). The last book offers a unified, coherent, and understandable view of the evolution of a neurotic character structure and what needs to be undone to help a person more constructively develop potentials toward becoming his or her "real self."

In my analytic training at the American Institute for Psychoanalysis, Horney was my teacher and faculty adviser. The basic tenets of what I learned included those that Horney had learned from Freud and still included in her beliefs, and those tenets that came from her own evolving ideas that differed from his. Important to us were the beliefs that included:

1. What is not in our awareness resides in our unconscious;
2. As Freud so clearly delineated, dreams are the royal road to what is unconscious, though the dream symbols are not to be rigidly interpreted, as their meaning varies with changing context, time, places, feelings, free-associations, and manifest as well as latent implications of the dreamer, who is the architect of his or her own dream and is represented by "all and everything" in the dream;
3. There is a powerful process moving our lives called psychic determinism;

4. The fact of our genetic inheritance, the actual events and environmental forces in our whole life, especially those of our early years as well as the cultural and social factors in our lives. All influence the degree to which we are healthy or neurotic;
5. Understanding that the process of "basic anxiety," which develops in childhood, is considered to be the "dynamic center of neurosis," and our culture generates a great deal of anxiety in each person. Basic anxiety can be defined as a sense of isolation, weakness, vulnerability, helplessness, abandonment, and confusion;
6. The analyst-patient relationship as being most important to experience, acknowledge, and attempt to understand and alter constructively during psychoanalytic treatment, which inherently includes disillusionment. In treatment we find the emergence of the repeated, characteristic multiple transferential projections and distortions that first develop in childhood and that hinder individuals from achieving their greatest potentials in their relationships throughout their lives, especially with authorities;
7. When we are confronted in our analytic work with what is classically referred to as resistance, we can best clarify and undermine such resistance to openness, change, and growth by joining the patient in unearthing "the nature of the blockage" and what forces have kept it going until now;
8. The existence of an "idealized image" each of us created in childhood out of the need to survive and the powerful drive to fulfill this impossible-to-achieve "idealized image." This nonfulfillment of an irrational, contradictory image in turn leads to the development of manifestations of "self-hate" and, conversely, when we momentarily do fulfill some aspect of this "idealized image" to short-lived feelings of neurotic pride. Giving up the image of who "we believe we should be," filled with its seething cauldron of excessive expectations, gives us the inner space, freedom, and energy to pur-

sue the multiple potentials lying dormant within on the road to becoming our own "real self."

9. By reducing alienation and distance from our potential authentic self and owning (which does not mean acting out) our feelings and thoughts, we can move toward becoming a more integrated, wholehearted, and satisfied human being when alone or with others.

Horney spoke of psychoanalysis in a loving fashion (1942a):

> I should like to speak of psychoanalysis tonight, not in a learned manner, but rather as a sailor speaks of his boat. He knows its deficiencies and its assets; and loves it regardless of any faults it may have. We are often inarticulate in attempting to explain why we love a person or thing, and may even have to pause to define the reason carefully.
>
> Why do I love psychoanalysis? At first I thought I loved it because it gave an interesting and sometimes an almost aesthetic pleasure. There is, for instance, a pleasure in analyzing a dream, in understanding its meaning, and in explaining it to a patient.
>
> Secondly, there is the therapeutic appeal of psychoanalysis. It can cure neurotic disturbances, such as alcoholism, depression, fears of various sorts, etc. And there is great satisfaction when we succeed in helping a patient to become healthy.
>
> These intellectual and therapeutic interests would intrigue me still today. But to stress them alone would appear to me like saying that you love a man because he is tall and handsome and has a nice voice, without considering other, deeper reasons why he is loved.
>
> Now I see that psychoanalysis is one of the most powerful aids in growth and development. It is true that we can develop as long as we live. Actually we take it for granted, but we neither accept it nor practice it. We seem to expect that growth and change occur only in children and adolescents. After that people tend to accept themselves as they are. There are many points at which development may halt, producing a variety of general types.

There are, for example, those who have sunk into conformity, lost their colorfulness and individuality, and become static in their development, thus failing to make the contribution to society, as well as to their own happiness, that they are potentially capable of making. Others develop a drive for power; there are many little Hitlers going about in society. Another type is formed by those who become rigidly perfectionistic and develop a moral smugness. Still others are motivated by prestige. They get more satisfaction from recognition than in doing the job well. We are too ready to accept others and ourselves as we are and to assume that we are incapable of change. Our general attitude toward age is that it is a period of rigidity and finality. We forget the idea of growth, or we do not take it seriously. There is no good reason why we should not develop and change until the last day we live.

Psychoanalysis is one of the most powerful means of helping us to realize this aim. It is a specific means of uncovering unconscious processes which are interfering with our development. Life itself is the best therapist, but it is ruthless, and does not ask how much a person can stand. In times like these, society needs individuals who are strong, courageous, warm, and cooperative. Every analyst feels gratified to help individuals, but he must also be concerned about all those in distress who cannot be reached in private practice.

The Fiftieth Anniversary Conference to honor the contributions of Karen Horney opened with Susan Quinn's presentation on "Awakened to Life: Sources of Independence in the Girlhood of Karen Horney." Susan Quinn is a prize-winning writer and evidenced her talents for thorough research and imaginative synthesis of information obtained in the exciting story she put together in *A Mind of Her Own: The Life of Karen Horney* (1978). In Part One of this book she presents enough details of Karen's life in childhood and adolescence with her family and peers at school to give us the foundation for the conclusions she draws in her conference paper regarding Horney's spirit of independence, her ability to take a minority position with tenacity, and her capacity to question what was real truth and what was myth or contemporary truth parading as ultimate truth. Quinn traveled to a number of continents to unravel the background and life story of Horney through information from family members, colleagues, and others.

From this more intimate account of Horney as a person by Susan Quinn we move to an overview of "Karen Horney's Feminine Psychology and the Passions of Her Time." Paradoxically, as Douglas Ingram points out in his discussion of this paper by Marianne Horney Eckardt, we learn about the intellectual and cultural currents of the times in which she lived and was influenced by from her daughter and learn more of the intimate details about Horney from Quinn, who did not know her in person but learned much about her. Marianne Eckardt, who has previously written about her mother's contributions to feminine psychology (1991) and to psychoanalytic theory, gives us additional insight into the pervasively repressing and restrictive attitudes toward women that surrounded Horney as she developed the strength to take a stance against this gender-based oppression. She links the revolt of women against tyranny by men with the rebellion of men against fathers and patriarchal domination and authoritarianism. Eckardt remarks on Karen Horney's unfailing instinct to be in the right place at the right time but also notes she had the spirit and creativity to make something of that opportunity.

Douglas Ingram, who has been intensely interested in the life and contribution of Horney, having edited in 1987 her 1952 *Final Lectures* at the American Institute for Psychoanalysis, integrates his reactions to the papers by both Quinn and Eckardt. Having a deep interest in philosophy and metaphors, he brings us into contact with Hegel, Nietzsche, and others who touch us in the domains of ethics, morality, and truth. He asks provocative questions and reminds us that whereas for Freud psychoanalysis was very much a science, Horney was unclear as to how psychoanalysis was a science and how it was art.

The presentation by Helen Singer Kaplan entitled "Does the New Liberated Woman Produce Impotency in Men?" (in this volume, entitled "The Myth of the New Impotence") attracted much interest and stirred up a lively interactive discussion with the audience. In answering the question, she brings forth her strong feelings that today there is no longer room for gender bias or gender blindness in examining the relationships between the two sexes. She emphasizes that she is talking as a humanist and not speaking from a feminist perspective. She focuses on similarities as well as differences in the sexualities, psyches, bodies, brains, and acculturation of men and women. She relates many examples that reveal the necessity to appreciate the systems involved in the interlocking relationships between males and females and the need for us to be "attuned to and embrace both the male and female view." Kaplan's extensive clinical experience reveal no scientific evidence that males have become "casualties of the sexual revolution which has brought greater freedom to women."

In his well-documented discussion of the presentation by Kaplan, Harold I. Lief speaks of Horney's "courageous stance" in writing "the initial dissenting views about female psychology, setting herself in opposition to Freud." Lief focuses on the challenge to the theory of universal penis envy by females and to the modern studies on orgasm, which indicate that it is not a sign of immaturity for women to experience and enjoy clitoral orgasm with or without accompanying vaginal orgasm. He agrees with the conclusions reached by Kaplan and adds that "if anything, the reverse is true—a sexually responsive woman at home with her body and confident of her responsivity is apt to help a frightened or inexperienced man overcome his anxieties." He refers us to the play *Tea and Sympathy* as an example of this.

Jean Baker Miller, who has directed the Stone Center for Developmental Services and Studies at Wellesley College since its inception in 1981, was the distinguished psychiatrist we chose to grace our podium and to give the 39th Annual Karen Horney Lecture. Her paper on "Women's Psychological Development: Connections, Disconnections, and Violations" moved the focus of our attention to those verbal and nonverbal communications that are characteristic of growth-fostering relationships and then to a description of nongrowth promoting relationships, which in fact lead to disconnections between people. She points to the violence that is done to individuals by forces that do not allow for connectedness, emotional and psychological authenticity, and intimacy. Hers is a different voice, a voice not shrill and attacking but rather a voice to engage us in looking at and redressing wrongs that have been committed by men and women functioning as stereotyped rather than as wholehearted humanistic and involved individuals. She exhorts women to urgently pursue a "historic mission: to examine, describe, and raise to their full value the realm of growth-fostering relationships" so that we can live in a society of mutual empowerment.

Carol Gilligan, Director of the Harvard Project on the Psychology of Women and Development of Girls and author of *In a Different Voice* (1982) was most appropriate as the woman to follow Jean Miller; there is such a profound connection in their work and direction to bring about enlightenment and change in the ways males and females have been relating until now. In her provocative presentation, Gilligan offers many poignant illustrations from her research, in various communications with adolescent girls, to awakening of gender differences as they journey beyond childhood. She explicates the multilevel feedback, which leads them toward confusion, conflicts, and cultural experiences of a "double-binding" nature and then in turn leads to disconnections between self and self and between self and others in relationships. She poetically leads us to listen to and to hear "voices that differ from accepted truths." Gilligan emphasizes her affinity and overlapping of ideas and work with Jean Baker Miller and condenses her message into the sentence that reads, "Paradoxically, girls are taking themselves out of relationships for the sake of relationships and self-consciously letting go of themselves."

In the February 12, 1992 *New York Times*, a front-page article by Susan Chira reported "Bias Against Girls Is Found Rife in Schools, With Lasting Damage." She was highlighting the findings of a study commissioned by the American Association of University Women Educational Foundation that had reviewed over 1,000 publications in the 1980s about girls and women. The study was done at Wellesley College by Dr. Jean Baker Miller. Among the conclusions reached by the researchers were:

1. Teachers pay less attention to girls.
2. Girls still lag in mathematics and science grades and tend not to pursue careers in math and science.
3. Reports of boys sexually harassing girls are on the increase.

4. Some tests remain biased against girls, which hurt their chances of getting scholarships.
5. Textbooks continue to ignore or stereotype females, and in school, girls learn little or nothing about some of their most pressing problems like sexual abuse, discrimination, and depression.
6. Teachers called on boys more often than girls, offered boys more detailed and constructive criticism, and allowed boys to shout out answers to questions but reprimanded girls for doing the same thing.

This report, available through the A.A.U.W. Educational Foundation, 1111 16th Street, N.W., Washington, D.C. 20038-4873, affirms the research and clinical findings presented in the papers by both Drs. Miller and Gilligan in this volume as to what leads to lowered self-esteem, depression, and alienation in adolescent girls and young women.

Dr. Silvia Olarte came to the conference to discuss the papers by Miller and Gilligan when Alexandra Symonds, who was to be the discussant, became ill and could not attend. Symonds has been a major spokeswoman in her own right on women's issues. In addition to her serving as Editor of "News for Women in Psychiatry," published by the Association of Women Psychiatrists, she has been writing on gender concerns since 1972 when she published "The Myth of Femininity" in the *American Journal of Psychoanalysis*. She has also written on expansiveness in success-oriented women; wives as professionals; emotional conflicts of career women; sexism in the family; and more recently on gender issues and Horney theory. She was missed.

Dr. Olarte credited Drs. Miller and Gilligan for the new parameters added by their work to help in our continuing attempt to understand "the vicissitudes of women's psychological development within a societal frame of reference that is patriarchal, hierarchical, and controlling of the sources of power." She talks of "the complexity in women's desire and struggle to integrate their evolving self within the context of relationships." Olarte echoes the theme of Miller and Gilligan in stating how the lack of empathy in relationship with men "leaves us still experiencing our initial overwhelming emotions for which we solicited empathy, plus anger about their response to us and confusion about our own experience. This confusion fosters doubt about our self-worth. We tend to blame ourselves and not to question the other's inability to empathize." She concludes with attention to the need as well as ways for women to hold on to who they are and what they know and to define their needs or wants in such a manner that a potentially disconnected relationship with the other might be transformed into a mutually enhancing relationship.

The conference ended with a discussion of the Miller and Gilligan papers by Dr. Mario Rendon, Editor of the *American Journal of Psychoanalysis*. He attempts to complement the contributions of Drs. Miller and Gilligan by drawing some comparisons between gender issues as seen by Freud and Horney. He addresses the question of how their own genders were reflected in the theories developed by both Freud and Horney. While Freud's views were based on a biological model of phallocentrism with the primacy of masculine libido and women relegated to a secondary position, he notes that Horney, while acknowledging biological differences between males and females, insisted on the indelible imprint of human relationships "and culture" on human character. He reminds us that the well-known early women disciples of Freud—namely Helene Deutsch, Marie Bonaparte, and Melanie Klein—"were by and large dutiful daughters," while Horney was "the first to openly rebel and break with dogmatic Freudianism." He tells us that in the Middle Ages one of the Catholic Church councils raised the question of whether women, like men, had a soul. Rendon, reminding us of the destruction of the earth and humanity done by men, then asks what he calls "the inverted question: Do men, like women, have a soul?" He concludes his remarks by telling us of Horney's approach to the question of measuring humanity, which was, he says, to "stress a relationship, a connection, in this case the connection to ourselves."

This book of papers commemorating Horney's contributions not only to women but to all humanity will hopefully stand as a milestone on the path of undermining "man's inhumanity to man," to women, and to children. This meeting was one to shed light on what has been blinding us as we gather strength to cut the chains and fetters and to allow what is human in each of us to emerge more fully with mutuality and respect.

MILTON M. BERGER, M.D
New York, April 4, 1992

REFERENCES

Eckardt, M. H. (1991). Karen Horney's feminine psychology: The passions of the times. *American Journal of Psychoanalysis, 51*(3), 235–243.

Gilligan, C. (1982). *In a Different Voice: Psychological Theory and Women's Development.* Cambridge, MA: Harvard University Press.

Horney, K. (1937). *The Neurotic Personality of Our Time.* New York: Norton.

Horney, K. (1939). *New Ways in Psychoanalysis.* New York: Norton.

Horney, K. (1942a). Dedication. *American Journal of Psychoanalysis, 35.* 99–100.

Horney, K. (1942b). *Self-Analysis.* New York: Norton.

Horney, K. (1945). *Our Inner Conflicts. A Constructive Theory of Neurosis.* New York: Norton.

Horney, K. (1946). *Are You Considering Psychoanalysis?* New York: Norton.

Horney, K. (1950). *Neurosis and Human Growth: The Struggle Toward Self-Realization.* New York: Norton.

Horney, K. (1967/1973). *Feminine Psychology,* H. Kelman et al. (Eds.). New York: Norton.

Horney, K. (1980). *The Adolescent Diaries of Karen Horney.* New York: Basic Books.

Horney, K. (1987). *Final Lectures,* D. Ingram (Ed.). New York: Norton.

Quinn, S. (1978). *A Mind of Her Own: The Life of Karen Horney.* New York: Summit Books.

Sayers, J. (1991). *Mothers of Psychoanalysis: Helene Deutsch, Karen Horney, Anna Freud, Melanie Klein.* New York: Norton.

WOMEN BEYOND FREUD

New Concepts of Feminine Psychology

1

Awakened to Life

Sources of Independence in the Girlhood of Karen Horney

SUSAN QUINN

There are three women who were very important in the writing of my biography of Karen Horney. Jean Baker Miller was the first person to mention Karen Horney's name to me, and it was her praise of Horney that led me some years later to find out more. Marianne Horney Eckardt, Karen Horney's daughter, was an important source in my research, as were her two sisters, Renate and Brigitte. She and Renate were also the moving forces behind the translation and publication of Karen Horney's girlhood diaries—a charming book called *The Adolescent Diaries of Karen Horney*, published in 1980. I considered the diaries to be the true mother lode of my book.

The third person who was important to me in writing the biography was Carol Gilligan, who read the book in manuscript. It was she who pointed out that I was in danger of being overly influenced by the received wisdom about Karen Horney's work. A standard way of dismissing Horney, in the "orthodox" psychoanalytic world, has always been to say that she was a wonderful clinician, very, very good with patients, but that she had no theory, she was not a thinker. To many of you, this may have a familiar ring: women are often dismissed in this fashion.

As I thought about this book honoring Karen Horney, it seemed important to acknowledge, right at the outset, the originality and the importance of the ideas of Karen Horney. And that has dictated the organization of this paper: I'll begin with Karen Horney's work, and then I'll move on to discuss her girlhood, and to search for clues, in those remarkable and revealing adolescent diaries, to the originality and independence of the woman she became.

I'll begin by saying that Karen Horney was, contrary to the received wisdom, an important thinker, an articulate writer, and a courageous teacher of her ideas. And because she was outspoken, because she broke with the reigning Freudians in 1941 and founded her own Institute, she has had her ideas appropriated over and over again without attribution. Historians of psychoanalysis have had to admit, however, that Karen Horney was very often there first. The psychologist David Rapaport points out that Karen Horney, in a 1936 paper called "The Problem of the Negative Therapeutic Reaction," anticipated Anna Freud's influential book, *The Ego and Mechanisms of Defense* (1966). "Horney really was the one who, possibly somewhat earlier than Anna Freud, pushed the investigation of defense mechanisms to the fore," he wrote, "justifiably so, because the psychoanalytic method . . . obliges the analyst to investigate both the unconscious material the patient prevents himself from communicating and the defense mechanisms by which he chooses to prevent . . . such communication" (Rapaport in Gill, 1967, p. 206).

Horney was also the first to write, vividly and at length, about narcissism. She referred to narcissism in different ways—"the pride system" was one term she used—but she was clearly talking about the constellation of behaviors now grouped under the rubric "narcissism." She wrote about it first in *The Neurotic Personality of Our Time* (1937) and subsequently in *Our Inner Conflicts* (1945) and *Neurosis and Human Growth* (1950). In addition, she suggested—as Heinz Kohut and Christopher Lasch did decades later—that it is *the* malady of modern times. The narcissistic character described by Heinz

Kohut, who goes through life seeking a sense of self through the affirmation of other people, is a very very close relative of the "false self" described by Horney in *Neurosis and Human Growth*, who emphasizes "appearing" over "being" (p. 38).

Furthermore, it is almost uncanny at times the degree to which her writings anticipate those of Heinz Kohut and the self-psychologists. Horney, writing in 1939 in *New Ways in Psychoanalysis*, asserted that the focus on the Oedipus complex in childhood tended to obscure the importance of "early relationships *in their totality* . . . such parental attitudes as having real interest in a child, real respect for it, giving it real warmth. . . . such qualities as reliability and sincerity" (pp. 86–87). Heinz Kohut, in an interview with me for a 1980 *New York Times Magazine* article, said, "I believe we have to very, very carefully re-evaluate . . . what has been so famous as the central conflict of human beings, the Oedipal conflict. . . . Is the Oedipal conflict really the normal issue that causes all our ills later? Or is it a disintegration product when parents fail to respond with pride and with empathy to their children's development?" (Quinn, 1980).

All the ideas I've discussed so far derive from the books Karen Horney wrote after she arrived in the United States in 1932. But the ideas that are most relevant to this book were propounded while she was still in Germany, in a series of 14 papers on the psychology of women (see Horney, 1967/1973). Taken together, they constitute a daring and persuasive counter to Freud's theory of female sexual development. Had she written nothing else, these papers would have earned Horney a place of importance in the history of psychoanalysis. But because she was expelled from the club in 1941, others who appropriated her ideas got more credit than she did. "It became an increasing trend in subsequent literature," Zenia Odes Fliegel noted in a 1972 article in the *Psychoanalytic Quarterly*, that ideas originating with Horney and supported by [Ernest] Jones were credited to Jones." And yet, as Fliegel notes, "in those early papers she [Horney] originated many ideas and observations which reappear in later writings on the subject—but in the fragmented and incomplete manner of the return of the repressed." It wasn't until 1967, when Harold Kelman compiled and translated them under the title *Feminine Psychology*, that these early essays began to be known and admired—most often by feminists who saw Horney as an early champion of their point of view.

I think there is no need to dwell on the phallocentric nature of Freud's view of female sexuality. I will quote briefly from "The Ego and the Id," just to remind you of how adamantly he insisted on the "primacy of the phallus." "The vagina is . . . valued," he wrote, "as a place of shelter for the penis" (Freud, 1961, p. 145). Some of his followers took up this phallocentrism with a vengeance. And one in particular, Karen Horney's own analyst Karl Abraham, presented a paper at the international meetings in 1920 in which he catalogued the many ways in which women spent their lives trying to compensate for the missing penis. Among his more comical assertions are that women's noses may swell up and become red because they—the noses—are responding as "a surrogate for the male genital" and that women's pleasure in "thrusting an umbrella into the ground" or in "using a hose for watering the garden" may be unconscious expressions of the childish wish for a penis (Abraham, 1922). It is probably almost too easy to laugh at this sort of thing now. But it was part of an overall devaluation of women that persisted in psychoanalysis for a long time and still persists in some circles.

In 1922, at a meeting chaired by Sigmund Freud and no doubt attended by her own analyst Karl Abraham, Karen Horney took issue with this phallocentrism and the inferiority of the female it implied. Her 1924 paper, called "On the Genesis of the Castration Complex in Women," was the first on female psychology given by a woman at an International Congress. It was a fairly mild dissent. There is one moment I love though, where she allows her indignation to bubble up: "We have assumed as an axiomatic fact," she writes, "that females feel at a disadvantage because of their genital organs . . . possibly because to masculine narcissism this seemed too self-evident to need explanation. Nevertheless, the conclusion so far drawn . . . amounting as it does to an assertion that one half of the human race is discontented with the sex assigned to it . . . is decidedly unsatisfying, not only to feminine narcissism but also to biological science" (Horney, 1924, p. 50).

Horney's second paper "The Flight from Womanhood" was far more ambitious and outspoken than her first. "How far," she asks, "has the evolution of women, as depicted to us today by analysis, been measured by masculine standards and how far therefore does this picture fail to present . . . the real nature of women?" (1926, p. 324). She proceeds, through the use of a chart, to demonstrate that the ideas that have been attributed to girls about their bodies in the psychoanalytic literature correspond, strikingly, to the ideas that *little boys* are likely to entertain about girls' bodies. For example, boys assume that little girls have a penis like theirs; girls are thought to believe they had a penis and to lament its loss. And so on. In other words, everything little girls are said to think is really what big boys think little girls think.

The bulk of Horney's essay is a protest against the joyless picture of female experience that psychoanalysis has painted. "What about motherhood," she asks rhetorically, and the "bliss" of bearing a new life, the "ineffable happiness" of expectation, the "joy" of the baby's arrival, the "deep pleasurable feeling" of nursing and caring for a new baby. In fact, Horney continues, turning the usual arguments upside down, motherhood gives women "a quite indisputable and by no means negligible physiological superiority." There is reason, in fact, for men to envy women! "Womb envy" was not Horney's phrase, but it was her concept.

As for penis envy, Horney concedes that it is readily observable in girl children—there is the "narcissistic mortification of possessing less than the boy" and also there are "manifest privileges" of having a penis—it is more visible and readily at hand for masturbation and urination.

But this childhood envy of the penis does not explain, in Horney's opinion, some women's tendency to disparage or flee from their femininity. The "flight from womanhood" of the title has two causes: one is anatomical, the other is social. Horney assumes that boys and girls have some awareness of their anatomy—of the vagina as well as the penis—from an early age. It is, she maintains, the girl's oedipal fantasy—the fear of penetration by a too-big penis—that causes her to recoil from her femininity with a mixture of guilt and anxiety (Horney, 1926). Similarly, as Horney would write in a remarkably empathic paper about male experience, it is the boy's fear of the disproportionate size of his penis in relation to his mother, and his fear of being swallowed up, which leads to the dread of women (Horney, 1932).

The second reason women flee from their femininity—and here we get to the theme which pervades all of Horney's work and makes it of a piece—the second reason is social. "The girl," she writes, "is exposed from birth onward to the suggestion . . . of her inferiority. . . . It seems to me," she concludes, "impossible to judge to how great a degree the unconscious motives for the flight from womanhood are reinforced by the actual social subordination of women" (Horney, 1926, pp. 69–70).

In the wake of "The Flight from Womanhood," Horney focused increasingly on this social reality—on the effects of the predominant "male culture" on the psychological lives of women. Later, she would cast off much of the biological focus of these early papers, which were given in what I call her Freudian period. But the stress on culture, which had helped her explain women's unhappiness with their lot, continued in the books she wrote after she crossed the Atlantic.

This brings me to the second part of my paper—the part which actually answers directly to the title, *Awakened to Life: Sources of Independence in the Girlhood of Karen Horney.* I hope you are convinced—if you weren't before you started to read this book—that Karen Horney was a remarkable, independent thinker. Now I'd like to ask why? What made her decide she would be a doctor before there were any medical schools in Germany admitting women? What made her decide to undergo psychoanalysis when it was still on the fringe? What was it, inherent or learned, in her childhood, that led her to be the first, within psychoanalysis, to take issue with Freud's ideas about women? And what was it, later on, that propelled her toward a break with the Freudians of the New York Psychoanalytic Society and led to the founding of the Karen Horney Psychoanalytic Center?

The phrase "Awakened to Life" is the title of a poem Karen Horney—then Karen Danielsen—wrote at age 18 after falling in love for the first time:

> Till now chasing after happiness in every form—now exultant happiness, heavenly joy in my heart.
>
> Till now only half alive with the constant, reproachful ques-

> tion in my eyes of whether this is really living, this everlasting monotony? Now full, whole life, joy of life in my veins down to the littlest fingertip. (Horney, *Diaries*, 1980, pp. 67–68)

The idea of the poem, of course, is that she is now living intensely for the first time, thanks to love. She is "awakened to life." But *my* point in using the phrase is that Karen Danielsen, born outside Hamburg in 1885, was awakened to life, absolutely aquiver with life, right from the beginning. Even in her baby picture, taken around two, her face shows a keen interest in the event of the photograph.

Her intensity is evident in the pages of her diary. She is madly in love with her teacher Herr Schulze long before she meets a boy closer to her own age. Then she thinks she shall "die of enthusiasm" over her French teacher, Fraülein Banning. She punctuates her accounts of school, of her reading, of a performance by Sarah Bernhardt, with multiple exclamation marks. And this intensity continued throughout her life—it wasn't just adolescent excess. Once, in her sixties, after seeing a movie with a woman friend, she was so upset by the friend's comment about the film that she walked off without her and hailed a cab, leaving the friend standing in the rain. Not very nice—you might say—but definitely intense.

Karen was born with unusual intelligence. She knew from early on that she was smart—smarter than her brother Berndt. "It was always my pride," she wrote in her diary, "that in school I was better than Berndt" (Horney, Diaries, 1980, p. 252). When a *Gymnasium* opened in Hamburg, just in the year that Karen came of age to go, she despaired that she might not be able to because of her father's reservations. "It brings me almost to the point of cursing my good gifts," she wrote in her diary (Horney, Diaries, 1980, p. 26). But she knew she had the gifts—and eventually she and her mother convinced her father to let her go. This native intelligence is a key ingredient, I think, in Karen's ability to be original: it allowed her to negotiate the academic aspect of medical school, where she was one of the few women, with relative ease.

Later, in Berlin, it made her quick to understand psychoanalysis: Karl Abraham wrote to Freud in 1912, "At our last meeting we enjoyed a report from Dr. Horney about sexual instruction in early childhood. For once, the paper showed a real understanding of the material, unfortunately something rather infrequent in the papers of our circle" (Abraham & Freud, 1965, p. 114). In 1932, when she came to the United States at age 47, her intelligence enabled her to quickly acquire fluency in English, to write her five theoretical books in English, and to become an enormously popular lecturer in English at the New School. Others were still struggling to pass the exam; some never did.

In young Karen Danielsen, this native ability and intensity were coupled with a strong independence of mind. This independence, which appeared early, may have grown out of her family situation. Karen was the second child born to Berndt Wackels and Clothilde Danielsen; the first child, Berndt, was three and a half years her senior. Her father was a sea captain of Danish origin, a widower with four grown children by a previous marriage when he married her mother. He was a zealous Lutheran who preached hellfire and brimstone around the house and—according to Karen's diary—made her mother miserable in the process.

Fortunately—as Karen notes, the zealous father was rarely home—his dangerous sea voyages around the cape of South America took him away frequently for six-month intervals. Karen and her brother Berndt depended on their mother for parenting. But their mother was deeply unhappy—often telling them that she lived only for them and would flee her marriage, even kill herself, if it weren't for them. When the sea captain was home, there were frequent quarrels, with Karen, her brother, and her mother on one side and her father and his children from the first marriage on the other.

Thus Karen was in many ways a parentified child who, like many modern children of divorce, felt she must take care of the distressed parent. "Mother is ill and unhappy," she wrote in her diary. "How miserable you feel when you see your loved ones suffer" (Horney, Diaries, 1980, p. 19). Because her father was a Lutheran, and allied with the overbearing pastor of the church, her anger toward the church and her father got entangled. "Today I read in a book that one should honor one's father not for his personal characteristics but to honor the authority God has vested in him. But it is awfully difficult" (Horney, Diaries, 1980, p. 22). By the time of her confirmation, she wrote in her diary that she "professed belief in the teachings of Christ, the doctrine of love, with hatred in my heart" (Horney, Diaries, 1980, p. 37). Later this same habit of questioning authority—her father and God the father—carried over into school, where she risked alienating her great crush, Herr Schulze, by doubting the resurrection. The urge and even the need to question authority never left her.

And yet, it is more complicated than that. She also wished to believe: "I long for the faith, firm as a rock that makes oneself and others happy" (Horney, Diaries, 1980, p. 38). This longing persisted too: at the end of her life she traveled to Japan to visit Zen monasteries.

It is perhaps not too farfetched to suggest that the wish for faith was partly a wish for closeness with her father. Because Karen Danielsen lived in a divided home, she was forced to take the side of her primary caretaker, her mother. Therefore, in her diary, she never expresses any positive feelings for her father. But I think she identified with him in important ways.

Later in life, Karen Horney told several people that she had traveled to South America with her father at age nine. But there are many reasons to doubt this. It was a six-month trip, on which she would have been the only female in the company of about 40 rough-and-ready sailors. And it was a very dangerous trip in those early days, one which her mother would probably have forbidden. But as Freud has observed in an essay on Leonardo da Vinci, "What someone thinks he remembers about childhood can cloak priceless pieces of evidence about the most important features of his mental development" (Freud, 1957, p. 84). And that's true here. Whether she went to South America on her father's boat or not, Karen Horney liked that idea. She imagined impossible worlds for herself. She loved the adventure stories of Karl May, a German who set his books in the American Wild West. With her friends, she acted them out, playing the part of Winnetou, the wise, wild Indian. Her diaries are full of her wish to experience the new, to break boundaries. "I am enthusiastic about everything new," she explains in the very first sentence of her diary (Horney, Diaries, 1980, p. 3). At 17, she writes that "an all-powerful longing seized me, almost bursting my breast, and it drove me forth to wander in order to *see*, to *enjoy* and to know all" (Horney, Diaries, 1980, p. 56). Sometimes, she imagined herself in places that were realistically beyond her: she planned to study medicine before medical school was open to women.

* * *

At this point in preparing this paper, I began to become distinctly uncomfortable with the argument I was constructing, brick by brick. It occurred to me that each of the qualities and each of the circumstances of Karen Danielsen's girlhood—the intensity, the intelligence, the dictatorial but adventurous father, the needy mother, could have made Karen Horney the original she became. Or they could have condemned her to a life of quiet desperation. Reading the tea leaves, after we know how the life turns out, is too easy. How many girls, intelligent and intense, were discouraged from higher education by their fathers, as Karen was, and simply gave up? And how many, enraged by their bullying fathers, didn't have the courage to fight back, directly or indirectly, against other authority figures? And as for Karen's relationship with her needy mother, that would seem to militate *against* ambition. Children who are consumed by the need to take care of a parent take a safe and sensible route. For Karen, as for most girls of her generation, that would have meant going to a women's teacher's college and settling for a modest income and a single life.

Yet here is Karen at age 16 planning to travel to Paris by herself (she didn't do this) and to spend a couple of years as a teacher before becoming—despite evidence of its utter impossibility—a doctor. Because the timing was right, and universities did open their door a crack to women by the time she finished *Gymnasium*, Karen did fulfill that dream.

But the point is that nothing in her childhood *dictates* that it would turn out this way. And so, at this juncture in the paper, I'm going to concede that individual development is a mystery. There is no way of really knowing why Karen Horney turned out the way she did.

What I can do is what biographers, therapists, and researchers alike do in contemplating a life or lives. They look for patterns, patterns that begin in childhood and repeat in various forms over a lifetime. In Karen Horney's life I see several that seem important to understanding how she grew.

First, there is the lifelong habit of introspection, of "listening," as she put it in her diary, "to the delicate vibration of my soul" (Horney, Diaries, 1980, p. 102). The second habit, linked to the first, is that she seemed to do her most creative and exhaustive self-exploration—and later writing for others—after she had experienced a loss or a rejection.

The most wonderful example of this occurs when, as a *Gymnasium* student, she tries to enroll in a course in dissection. She is turned down, for unclear reasons but probably because she is female. In her diary, she writes that instead of dissecting animals, she will "take myself to pieces. That will probably be more difficult, but also more interesting" (Horney, Diaries, 1980, p. 53). It is a statement that shines like a beacon into her future.

Lengthy self-examination frequently followed rejection. After she broke up with Rolf, her first serious boyfriend, she wrote a very long, blow-by-blow account of the relationship, trying to understand where it failed. The writing itself, on this occasion and I think on subsequent occasions, was a self-consoling activity as well as an intellectual one.

Similarly, when her marriage ended in 1926, her writing activity accelerated. Between 1926 and 1932, she wrote more articles than at any other time in her life—including not only those about female sexuality but others more directly related to the breakup, on marriage, and on the distrust between the sexes.

In a similar way, I think that Karen Horney's analysis was the disappointment, or one of them, that led to her later departure from libido theory. In 1910, when Karen Horney entered treatment with Karl Abraham, Freud's disciple, psychoanalysis was ill-prepared to deal with such an unrepressed woman. At around the same time that Freud was writing that respectable women do not violate the prohibition against sex before marriage, Karen Horney was violating the prohibition. The result was a bad fit—an analyst who was trying to free the libido and an analysand whose libido was already free and who had other reasons for her unhappiness.

We know a little about her analysis—once again from those wonderful diaries. We know that she was deeply depressed when she entered analysis. And from the entries, we can gather that Abraham focused a great deal of attention on Horney's oedipal attachment to her father. "Dr. A. thinks," she writes in her diary, that "I got my erotic ideal" from the "time when I loved my father with all the strength of my passion." This in turn explains her attraction to "brutal and rather forceful men" and therefore her discontent with her rather mild husband, who is her *conscious* choice but doesn't meet her unconscious needs (Horney, Diaries, 1980, p. 230).

There may be *something* to this. But not much. My guess is that it really misses the mark in Karen Horney's case. Another early Abraham analysand, Sandor Rado, has said that analysis in those early days "was not the study of the life of a person . . . it was a search for opportunities to apply certain Freudian insights—castration complex, narcissism, oral eroticism, anal eroticism."*

This seems to be true of Horney's analysis. Instead of focusing on repressed oedipal feelings, it might have been more useful to seek the roots of the "desperate loneliness" that so often afflicted Karen Horney. In her childhood, what was missing was probably more important than what had been repressed. What seems to have been left out of the exploration is the powerful reality of her father's *absence* during much of her childhood. He was away for many months at a time and distant and inaccessible when he was home. If there was a strong attraction, there must also have been strong feelings of disappointment, abandonment, even rage. And her mother's unhappiness must have contributed as much or more to her lost, lonely feelings.

The result of this bad fit between Karen Horney and early psychoanalysis was that Horney ended her analysis dissatisfied. And that dissatisfaction, in turn, led to her departure 30 years later from the biologically based drive theory that had dominated her treatment.

Finally, Karen Horney reacted to her demotion and the resulting split at the New York Psychoanalytic in 1941 by developing, more forcefully than before, an independent Horneyan theory. *The Neurotic Personality of Our Time* (1937) and *New Ways in Psychoanal-*

---

*From interviews with Sandor Rado, 1964–1965, conducted by Bluma Swerdloff for the Oral History Research Office of Columbia University.

ysis (1939) reacted to Freudian theory. Her last two books, written after the split, *Our Inner Conflicts* (1945) and *Neurosis and Human Growth* (1950), really laid out an alternative theoretical framework. I believe that in many ways the split was unfortunate—it isolated Horney from the orthodox group, and they could have used each other. And it is, as I said earlier, the main reason her work is still not given as much credit as it deserves. But I suspect that Horney's last two books—written following a rejection—would not have been as original had she stayed in the "orthodox" fold.

Here I come to the end of my exploration of the roots of Horney's originality. On balance, I would tend to attribute a lot to mysterious inborn qualities—her intensity, her intelligence. The habit of questioning authority, the ability to imagine impossible worlds for herself, the tendency to respond to loss with introspection and analysis—in writing—and the particularly unsettled nature of her childhood and adolescence that placed her at odds with Freudian wisdom, all these things contributed to her originality. But in the end, none of these inborn or learned characteristics would have mattered if Karen Horney didn't have a sense of her life's possibilities, an excited feeling about herself that couldn't be dampened by all the obstacles society put in her way. And here I think we must give credit to her mother, who always supported and encouraged her ambitions. At age 18, Karen Horney wrote in her diary, "Strange, that it is so infinitely difficult for me to convince myself that I am something ordinary, an average person, one of the herd" (Horney, Diaries, 1980, p. 65). Fortunately for us, Karen Horney never did convince herself of that.

REFERENCES

Abraham, H.C., & Freud, E.L. (Eds.) (1965). *Letters of Sigmund Freud and Karl Abraham 1907–1926*. New York: Basic Books.

Abraham, K. (1922). Manifestations of the female castration complex. *International Journal of Psycho-analysis 3* (1), 1–29.

Fliegel, Z.O. (1972). Feminine psychosexual development in Freudian theory.*Psychoanalytic Quarterly, 12*, 385–408.

Freud, A. (1966). *The Ego and Mechanisms of Defense.* Madison, CT: International Universities Press.

Freud, S. (1957). Leonardo da Vinci and a memory of his childhood. In J. Strachey (Ed. and Trans.), *The Standard Edition of the Complete Psychological Works of Sigmund Freud* (Vol. 11, p. 84). London: Hogarth Press.

Freud, S. (1961). The ego and the id. In J. Strachey (Ed. and Trans.), *The Standard Edition of the Complete Psychological Works of Sigmund Freud* (Vol. 19, p. 145). London: Hogarth Press.

Gill, M. (Ed.) (1967). *The Collected Papers of David Rapaport.* New York: Basic Books.

Horney, K. (1924). On the genesis of the castration complex in women. *International Journal of Psycho-analysis*, 5, 50–65. (also in K. Horney, 1967/1973, *Feminine Psychology,* H. Kelman et al. [Eds.])

Horney, K. (1926). The flight from womanhood. *International Journal of Psycho-analysis*, 7, 324–339 (also in K. Horney, 1967/1973, *Feminine Psychology,* H. Kelman et al. [Eds.]).

Horney, K. (1932). The dread of woman: Observations on a specific difference in the dread felt by men and women for the opposite sex. *International Journal of Psycho-analysis, 13*, 348–360. (also in K. Horney, 1967/1973, *Feminine Psychology,* H. Kelman et al. [Eds.]).

Horney, K. (1937). *The Neurotic Personality of Our Time.* New York: Norton.

Horney, K. (1939). *New Ways in Psychoanalysis.* New York: Norton.

Horney, K. (1945). *Our Inner Conflicts. A Constructive Theory of Neurosis.* New York: Norton.

Horney, K. (1950). *Neurosis and Human Growth. The Struggle Toward Self-Realization.* New York: Norton.

Horney, K. (1967/1973). *Feminine Psychology,* H. Kelman et al. (Eds.). New York: Norton.

Horney, K. (1980). *The Adolescent Diaries of Karen Horney.* New York: Basic Books.

Quinn, S. (1978). *A Mind of Her Own: The Life of Karen Horney.* New York: Summit Books.

Quinn, S. (1980). Oedipus vs. Narcissus (personal interview with Heinz Kohut). *New York Times Magazine*, November 9.

2

Karen Horney's Feminine Psychology and the Passions of Her Time

MARIANNE HORNEY ECKARDT, M.D.

The time was the 1920s, when the short, fateful span of the Weimar Republic engendered creative flamboyance as well as political and economic turmoil. The place was Berlin, then considered the most exciting, cosmopolitan city of the West. There Karen Horney began her lifelong challenge of Freudian theory by writing a series of papers on feminine psychology and marriage. Collected long after her death, these papers were edited by Harold Kelman and published in 1967 under the title *Feminine Psychology.* In the 1970s, feminists hailed the book and proclaimed Karen Horney an early champion of their cause. They believed that the papers were pioneering in their rejection of the phallocentric psychoanalytic view of women. Seen against the background of Horney's own time, however, these essays acquire a different significance. I will try to illuminate this background, the currents of her time.

A brief summary of the content and style of these early papers is useful. From the perspective of Horney's contributions to psychoanalysis, the articles on feminine psychology can be viewed as stepping stones in the evolution of her own theories of neurotic development, which she presented in five books between 1937 and 1950. Many aspects of early psychoanalytic theory troubled her, among them Freud's glaring discriminatory differentiation between male and female psychological development. The issue provided a good starting focus for her critical, inquiring mind, leading her to recognize the pivotal importance of cultural factors in personality development, of the conflicts these factors spawned, and of the dynamics they generated. Once she saw her way clear to severing her umbilical ties to the libido theory, any reference to feminine psychology disappeared. In her mind, the dynamics of men's neurotic development were the same as women's.

In 1922 Horney launched her challenge to Freud's vision of the inequality of the sexes by responding to Karl Abraham's paper "The Manifestations of the Female Castration Complex" with her article "On the Genesis of the Castration Complex in Women." In this paper she disputes Abraham's assumption that females feel at a disadvantage because of their genital organs. Is male narcissism, she wonders, responsible for the belief that half of the human race is discontented with its sex? This theory does not seem to be good biological science. In her practice, Horney had frequently encountered symptoms of penis envy or the wish to be a man. Do such symptoms or wishes, she wonders, derive solely from coveting a penis? Subsequent writings emphasize that our culture is masculine in nature—that the very standards by which mankind estimates the value of male and female are masculine ones. She asks many big questions. Why has motherhood been depreciated? Does the man's greater cultural productivity arise partly from his feeling that he plays a relatively small role in the creation of living beings and is thus compelled to overcompensate through achievements and mastery? The basic struggle between the sexes and the denial of this struggle became the theme of four significant papers.

These essays make fascinating reading. In a lively style, Horney poses clear questions and uses clinical vignettes to illustrate theoretical issues. She takes us back in time and allows us to participate in her journey of exploration. We find ourselves in a psychoanalytic world where such issues as castration, the presence or absence of a penis, penis or womb envy, and the denial of the vagina are discussed with a literalness and intensity alien to us in the 1990s. Psychoanalysis was a young science, and the atmosphere in Berlin was one of excitement and debate. We know that Horney's struggles to become an emancipated woman and her experience of conflicts in marriage lent passion to her inquiry and argumentations.

Horney's journey took place amid the currents and passions of her time. The turn of the century—almost literallly the year 1900—opened new vistas to women. To appreciate the accomplishments of our century, we must remember the imposing bondage of restrictions that then existed. Women had no voting rights in Germany until the demise of the old empire and its constitution in World War I. Women were denied access to higher education. In 1901, Heidelberg and Freiburg became the first universities to open their doors to women; the University of Berlin reluctantly followed in 1908. The decree admitting women in Prussia implied that except for unusual individuals, women were incapable of teaching subjects in which reason rather than emotion was the criterion of competence. Discrimination pervaded all civil legislation. But women were not the only ones struggling against the heavy boot of Germany's authoritarian culture. We will see that the changing place of women became intimately linked to the rebellion of sons against fathers—to a male revolt against authoritarianism, science, and the rational mind designed to liberate in men the creative force, the imagination, the source of emotion, the senses, and the erotic. This revolt freely used the designations "masculine" and "feminine" as metaphors for the two poles. Although Horney's papers do not reflect the then-current dialogue about masculine and feminine, they do contain prevalent questions about the morality of monogamy, the inevitable struggle between the sexes, the masculine view of our civilization, and the need to understand the real sources of our struggles.

Karl Kraus's conception of womanhood exemplifies some of the essential vocabulary of the movement. In 1899, Kraus, a brilliant satirist living in Vienna, began publishing his fortnightly paper *Die Fackel* ("The Torch"), which he wrote singlehandedly until 1936. In it, he sought to expose the moral duplicity and hypocrisy of Viennese society. Although it spared no one, his sharp, biting wit had a moral base. He considered prostitutes and homosexuals victims of this hypocrisy and rallied to their support. His writings about women reflect the bias typical of his time: women and men are radically different types of beings. Woman's essence is sexuality. Although man has sexual urges, woman is sexuality itself. She is emotion and irrationality and cannot be expected to control her nature.

Kraus was influenced by the writings of Otto Weininger, who published his controversial book *Sex and Character* in 1903. Weininger based his views on the notion that the concepts masculine and feminine represent psychological ideal types and do not exist in pure form, but they help to explain human behavior. The masculine idea is perfect rationality and creativity. The feminine idea is pure wanton urge. The essence of womanhood is universal fecundity, the source of all irrationality and chaos in the world. Men and women are androgynous, and the two ideal types appear in them in varying proportions. All positive achievements derive from the masculine principle, all that is destructive from the feminine principle. At his most extreme, Weininger declares that the Aryan race is the very embodiment of the masculine-creative principle of being, while the Jewish race and culture represent the feminine-chaotic principle of nonbeing. Jewish himself, Weininger was considered the epitome of Jewish self-hatred.

Weininger and his book are a phenomenon that interests the psychiatrist. Read today, his work reflects mainly the author's psychopathology. That the intellectuals of his time took his book seriously enough to make it a staple in their libraries seems incomprehensible. His categories of maleness and femaleness are defined by good and bad. Anything bad in man or woman is female, everything good is male. His anti-female statements are clearly linked to his personal battle with his Jewishness. Nevertheless, the intelligentsia of his time were intrigued by his categories and used them to express their own very different interests.

A critical biographer of Weininger, Carl Dallago, suggested that while Weininger had his categories right, he failed to understand that the "nothingness" essential to woman is one aspect of the Kierkegaardian abyss into which one must leap to find truth. Kraus agreed with Dallago. In Kraus's view, male and female are characterological categories. The essence of woman (the female principle) is a tender fantasy, the unconscious origin of everything worthwhile in human experience. It is the source of inspiration and creativity. Reason is merely a technique, a means by which men obtain what they desire. The feminine fantasy fertilizes the masculine reason and gives it direction. Thus the source of moral and aesthetic truth is the unity between feeling and reason, which are complementary sides of the same coin.

Kraus sees the encounter between man and woman as the "origin" in which reason is fertilized by the wellspring of fantasy. This encounter results in creativity and a moral integrity that expresses itself in everything a person does. From this moral stance, Kraus lashes out, attacking everyone and everything, including the feminist movement and psychoanalysis. He abhorred the feminist desire to create women with masculine aims, women who wish to be like men. He chided psychoanalysis for its lopsided view of sexuality. Psychoanalysis, he believed, created a further imbalance between masculine and feminine, reason and fantasy, conscious and unconscious. Kraus would have chosen to return to childhood with Jean Paul rather than with Sigmund Freud, because Jean Paul envisioned childhood as a time when fantasy vivifies everything we do, while Freud saw it as a series of crises resulting in frustrations.

The notions of feminine and masculine principles find a less intellectual outlook—a drama of passions and deep beliefs—in the fascinating saga of Otto Gross (Green, 1974). Gross moved from Graz, Austria, to Munich, where he studied medicine and later psychiatry. After working as an assistant at Emil Kraepelin's clinic in 1905, he became an early psychoanalyst, impressing Freud and Jones with his brilliance. Gross's circle encompassed Frieda Lawrence (before her marriage to D. H. Lawrence) and her sister Else Jaffe, who in turn was close to Max and Marianne Weber and the intellectural elite of Heidelberg.

Gross became a leading exponent of the ideological revolution that arose across Europe between 1890 and 1910. Its adherents viewed eroticism as a philosophical value—as life-creating. Indeed, the new ideas were considered the major hope of resistance to patriarchal civilization. The anti-patriarchal feeling was partly a reaction to Otto von Bismarck's Prussia, a country that exaggerated the patriarchal elements in Western Europe to become a caricature of the patriarchal male. In his personal life, Gross was subjected to a narrowly autocratic father, a criminal judge who imposed his will at home with a punitive hand. Gross and his circle believed in free love—love that was free of social restrictions, possessiveness, and jealousy and was the necessary precursor of full love in a relationship. Although Gross attracted outstanding writers to his circle, many became disenchanted because his charismatic brilliance was marred by morphine and cocaine addiction and because his anarchistic beliefs too often created destructive dramas.

The new erotic freedom was considered a new matriarchal morality. Such old values as chastity and fidelity, self-sacrifice and denial, were regarded as moralistic corruptions of moral feelings. This phenomenon is best understood by examining the immediate predecessor of Gross's circle. Members of the Cosmic Circle, also based in Munich, met regularly between 1897 and 1903 to discuss mythology, anthropology, and cultural history and developed a *Weltanschauung* radically opposed to that of the patriarchal Western civilization. They too believed in eroticism and the value of myth and primitive cultures. They proclaimed the superiority of instinct and intuition over the values of science and espoused the primacy of the female mode of being. They quoted J. J. Bachofen (Bachofen, 1964) more often than Nietzsche and revived and embraced the ideas Bachofen set forth in his book *Mutterrecht*, published in 1854. Born to a patrician family in Basel, Switzerland, Bachofen was perturbed by the violence of the 1848 revolution and feared for the heritage of European culture. He imaginatively reconstructed this heritage, investigated Roman antiquities, and believed he had found traces of earlier matriarchal cultures. He theorized that matriarchal forms of society preceded patriarchal ones everywhere. Characteristic of these primitive societies was a social organization that protected life and love, penalizing all injuries to physical life, both animal and human. The greatest crime was matricide. This matriarchal, lunar phase then evolved into the solarian phase, civilized culture as we know it, which is characterized by father-rights, division of labor, and individual ownership.

Although Bachofen makes interesting reading, we must remember that the Bachofen ideas being embraced around 1900 reflect him as little as Weininger's writing reflected the appropriated concepts of male and female principles. A philosopher of history rather than an anthropologist, Bachofen sought universal laws of history and believed he had found them in myths and in the myths of religion. He saw in religion man's effort to free himself from the bonds of this earth and viewed the struggle of polar forces as the source of all creativity and greatness. As an evolutionist, Bachofen believed in the progress of the simple toward the complex, in the evolution of the simpler form of matriarchy into the more complex form of patriarchy.

Bachofen also maintained that the relationship at the origin of all culture—of every virtue and of every noble aspect of existence—is that between mother and child. In a world of violence, it operates as the divine principle of love, of union, and of peace. Progress from the maternal to the paternal conception of man is the most important turning point in the history of the sexes. As begetter, the father had no visible relation to the child. With the triumph of paternity came the liberation of the spirit from the manifestations of nature, a sublimation of human existence over the laws of material life. Man became conscious of his higher calling, and spiritual life superseded corporeal existence. The myth of triumphant paternity is represented as partaking of heavenly light. As the divinity of the mother yields to the divinity of the father, night cedes to day, the left side to the right. Spiritual development, individualism, and acceptance of transcendence over nature arise. Mankind owes the enduring victory of paternity to Roman law, which made it the foundation of all life and protected it from the decadence of religion, the corruption of manners, and the popular return to matriarchal views.

Bachofen's appeal lay in his nostalgic descriptions of aspects of matriarchy. He described the matriarchal period as the poetry of history because of the sublimity, the heroic grandeur, even the beauty to which women rose by inspiring bravery and chivalry in men. Matriarchal states were notably free from internal strife and permeated by an air of tender humanity. Equally appealing was his idea that history recorded a stratification of spiritual modes, allowing us to appreciate what no longer exists.

Bachofen's ideas had little effect until the turn of the century rediscovered him. The best-known figures of the Cosmic Circle were Ludwig Klages, Karl Wohlskehl, and at times Stefan George. Klages believed that soul and body were the two poles of natural life in man and that he who works by abstraction and logic—who reifies and fixes the movement of this polarity—creates an artificial world of concepts that is hostile to life.

I hope it is clear that the popularity of the terms "matriarchy," "woman," "femininity," and "eros" had little to do with real concern for women. Many protagonists of the erotic movement were neither particularly erotic nor necessarily fond of women. However, the rhetoric of the female principle as representing a greater capacity for connectedness was prevalent.

Gross's psychoanalytic writings are of interest because they express the ideal of self-realization, a concept dear to Horney's later works. He writes in 1907, when he was in Berlin, that psychoanalysis is called upon to make men capable of freedom and to create a ferment of revolt within the psyche against the dominant ego. We have the ability to know ourselves, and once we do, we realize that what we are is only a fraction of our full psychic potential. We are fragmented by conflicts that manifest themselves in our sexual lives. These conflicts derive from the impositions of the outside world on the individual—impositions introjected in childhood in the form of authority. Society's original sin is enslaving women. Today's revolutionary fight is against father and patriarchy, while tomorrow's is the revolution for matriarchy (Green, 1974).

In her early papers, Horney refers enthusiastically to the writings of social philosopher Georg Simmel (Simmel, 1984). A less flamboyant figure than Gross, Simmel taught at the University of Heidelberg and was undoubtedly influenced by the Cosmic Circle and its *Lebensphilosophie* (life philosophy). Simmel describes Western civilization as masculine: the state, the laws, morality, religion, and the sciences are the creation of men. Further, the very standards by which mankind has estimated the value of male and female nature are in themselves masculine. The concept of human being is equated with the concept of man. Horney felt that Simmel's views affirmed her notions that women were not seen in their own right.

Reading Georg Simmel now, one can only be disappointed. His

style is dry and academic. He does write about the masculine nature of our civilization, but he has doubts about women's potential to contribute. Women's strength is their refined sensitivity and vulnerability. Their periphery is more closely connected to their center, and its aspects are more completely integrated into the whole. Women have a greater fidelity to values, but they are vulnerable to diversity, which alienates and destroys them. A productive culture, however, is manifested by its diverse specialization. The ability to function in diversity requires a detachment characteristic of man but not of woman.

Simmel leaves one grappling with many ambiguities. He declined to consider whether the masculine character of our culture results from the inner nature of the sexes or from male dominance. What is relevant to my theme is that Simmel, too, follows the prevalent rhetoric of the essential masculine and feminine nature and its effect on culture.

Summarizing some of the trends evidenced in these male writings or male-initiated movements, we can state that the latter part of the nineteenth century witnessed a shift in the stereotypical rhetoric about the essence of male and female nature. In the rebellion against reason, the negative attributes of women suddenly appeared in a positive light: they were considered more core-centered, intuitive, and sensitive. This view, however, was primarily men's new vision of reaching for their own souls, for the sources of their own imaginations. The liberation of Eros shifted the woman as the source of evil to a pedestal of strong earthy passion, which then nourished men. Although these currents were part of man's quest for his soul, they did heighten regard for women and prepared the way for women's entry into the world as equal partners.

How did pioneering women write then, and how did they differ? Swedish writer Ellen Key (Key, 1911), widely popular in Germany, was one of the pioneers, and she had a direct connection to Horney. At 18, Karen refers in her diary to Key and her book *On Love and Marriage*. "If sometime in later years I ask myself who in these years lit the sacred flame of enthusiasm for me, who was the lustrous star toward which my soul directed its way," Karen writes, "one name above all shines before me: Ellen Key. All I have been thinking about love and marriage in recent years, all I have won for myself in ardent battles, all this she sets before the world in radiant letters. What I saw and understood in mute forebodings, I see in her in bright daylight. . . . Ellen Key is a believer in life" (p. 53).

Ellen Key was born in Sweden in 1848 (Evans, 1976). Her father was active in Parliament as an avowed radical. His grandfather, a disciple of Jean Jacques Rousseau, had given the name Emile to his son, who in turn passed it on to his son. The name seemed to carry with it Rousseau's love for the natural and his ideas about education. Key's book *The Century of the Child*, published in 1909, is full of reverence for the healthy instincts of children. Key was hailed by the more liberal voices of the largely conservative women's movement in Germany. Because human beings had been defined as man par excellence, she believed that women should claim their place in the world as women. Society and the race were entitled to receive the best woman had to give. She sought a new morality centered on love, a morality more important than isolated reform measures. She questioned the morality of monogamy. She did not consider monogamy bad in itself, but felt that marriage should be by choice. Thus monogamy as it existed was a lie. Christianity hindered true sexual morality by making monogamy its only form. Real fidelity, she wrote, could arise only when love and marriage became equivalent terms. The relevant question is not whether a sexual relationship is the only one, but whether it is a balanced union in which the soul does not betray the senses nor the senses the soul.

Key gave considerable thought to children. In her view, children begotten from a sense of duty would be deprived of the nourishing influence of parents who were full of life and radiated happiness and love. The happiness of the individual is important to the enhancement of the race. Key's new morality endeavors to create a culture of mankind rather than a culture through mankind. Her romantic idealism receives its fullest expression in these words: "For the first time, the great fashioners of culture will be able to work in marble, instead of hitherto, being forced to work in snow" (Key, 1911).

Her message of a new and transforming morality found a very receptive audience in Karen. Her veil of innocence had been pierced by a dramatic and enlighteneing conversation in 1903, when she was 17. Not only did her friend Alice tell her the facts of life, revealing that girls in her circle allowed men to pick them up and sleep with them, but she added explanations of lesbian love, incest, and prostitution. Recording the conversation in her diary several months later, Karen casts Alice as sophisticated enlightener and herself as naive prude duly shocked that girls of her class would do the worst thing a girl could do. She felt overwhelmed by the "whole dreadful knowledge" she had received all at once. Soon, however, she rallied to investigate the subject further by walking the streets frequented by prostitutes and reading a book about prostitutes in Paris. She perused books by Emile Zola and other erotically informing works. Typically, she began digesting the information and asking questions. It is wrong for women to give themselves to men outside of marriage? She soon arrived at her answers. A woman who gives herself to a man she really loves is never immoral so long as she is prepared to bear the consequences. Karen embraced her answer with joyful certainty, asking herself where such certainty came from. Recalling Shakespeare's line "There is nothing either good or bad, but thinking makes it so," she writes: "One should base every consideration of things human on this sentence. A girl who gives herself to a man in free love stands morally way above the woman who, for pecuniary reasons or out of a desire for a home, marries a man she does not love. Marriage is something only external. It is bad—not theoretically—but when one comes to know how few marriages are really good ones. . . . All our morals and morality are either nonsense or immoral. Will it ever change? And how? And when?" She continues in good rhetorical style: "The dawn of a new time is breaking. I hope with all the strength of my young hope. Perhaps even the next generation will not know these battles, perhaps it will already be stronger than we are because more of them stem from the union of love. Perhaps more of the next generation will become mothers, true mothers, whose children are children of love. For how difficult it is today for a young girl to admit that she is having a child. The immorality of abortion will cease in that time—which perhaps will never come" (Horney, 1980). Key simply affirmed Karen's theories.

As we have noted, Key influenced some of the more radical German feminists who sought to legalize abortion, accord women equal rights in marriage, simplify divorce laws, give legal recognition to free marriage, improve the conditions of unmarried mothers, and disseminate contraceptives. One of the outstanding figures of this relatively small group was Helen Stoecker, who became an advocate of this new morality (Evans, 1976). She and Karen are seemingly hewn from the same wood. At a young age, Stoecker rebelled against a narrow-minded Calvinist home. Determined to educate herself by becoming a teacher, she went to Bern, Switzerland, to take a doctorate in literature because no German university then admitted women. Active in promoting women's access to higher education and the professions, she was one of the founders of the suffrage movement in 1902 and an influential leader in a new organization working to protect unwed mothers. The many prominent men in its membership enhanced its status and potential effectiveness. Stoecker also pursued the larger goal of reforming codes of sexual life. Reading the annals of the feminist movements in Germany, one is struck by the lack of cohesion, the constant fights among centers of activity in the different provinces, and their relative ineffectiveness. The contrast with the English women's movement is striking. English feminists were well organized, purposeful, and courageous; they chained themselves to the barricades and were willing to go to jail for their cause. No such spirit is recorded in Germany, where the liberal group was in the minority. Women's political activity was handicapped by repressive legislation. In Prussia, at least on paper, women were not allowed to join or form political organizations or be politically active until 1908, and a general bias against women was still very pervasive.

Frustrated by political bickering, Helen Stoecker often switched organizational loyalties; but her mission went beyond particular reforms. She believed that women should experience life completely. Her authority was her interpretation of Nietzsche, who exhorted women to live life to the fullest and to escape the narrow existence that bourgeois custom dictated to them. Nietzsche, writes Stoecker, sought to replace the old life-denying ascetic morality of the church fathers—who saw in sexual love something sinful and in women something lowly and impure—with the life-affirming morality that frees human beings from guilty consciences and sanctifies their love.

Like Ellen Key, Stoecker called this evolving ethos "The New

Morality" (*Die Neue Ethik*). Sexual activity, she felt, was a natural and self-evident right, and its moral content could be judged only from the motives behind it. Stoecker also aspired for the liberation of women. She did not want to destroy marriage, but she believed that the institution as it existed was just a shadow of a higher form of marriage. She wanted to lead men out of their thoughtless tyranny to a clearer insight and more genuine values. She welcomed Freud's psychoanalysis and became a member of the Berlin Psychoanalytic Society, founded in 1910 by Karl Abraham. She must have crossed Horney's path there, however casually. Then 25, just married, and newly arrived in Berlin, Horney was in her last year of medical school and was embarking on the road to her brilliant professional career by entering analysis with Karl Abraham.

The years 1914–1919 were overshadowed by World War I and its immediate aftermath. The disruption of the war, the chaos of defeat, the dissolution of the old empire, and the radical reforms of the new Weimar Republic were an incredible historical watershed. Crumbling pre-1900 institutions were demolished, and the younger, more vital prewar stirrings—the radical, good as well as bad, the creative—could all unfold with little to restrain them. Ellen Key, Helen Stoecker, Otto Gross, and Georg Simmel were part of the forces that prepared and fertilized the ground for the cultural pyrotechnics of the Weimar Republic.

Students who would fully appreciate the spirit and fundamentally unpolitical nature of Karen Horney's early papers—the freedom and excitement of asking large questions—must see them in their historical context. The turn of the century was ripe for change, for a renewal of spirit and soul, a new way of seeing life and expressing it. Freud's discovery of the unconscious was only one of many currents that opened new vistas and expressions. In the major political and economic disruptions of World War I, existing currents unfolded exuberantly in the absence of a defined culture. This blossoming was evident in music, painting, dance, architecture, theater, and film. Vital, brilliant, and irresistible, Berlin became the mecca of all this activity. The infectious excitement even embraced such intellectual institutions as the Berlin Psychoanalytic Institute. The atmosphere of the institute in Berlin was a far cry from that of the Vienna Institute, the high temple where Freud presided.

Although they appreciated Freud's discovery, Berlin psychoanalysts viewed psychoanalysis as a new science and considered themselves pioneers in a new field rather than guardians of the Holy Grail. They related to one another as innovators, each venturing into new directions. The atmosphere thus encouraged inquiry, and the inquiry was exciting.

As we know, however, this excitement, buoyancy, and creativity existed alongside horrendous political and economic turmoil. The Weimar Constitution did not arise from any consistent political ideology. From the start, it compromised with conservative old institutions like the military and industrialists, and it was fragmented by as many as 30 parties. It was a ludicrous caricature of the democratic process. Inflation, economic bankruptcy, and political chaos created an atmosphere of daily living with no foundation in past traditions and a totally uncertain future. The disorganized forms of the political game dampened any desire for participation. Books of the time reflect the tradition of a politically uninvolved intellectual elite who considered politics dirty and preferred expressing their ideas in the purity of an intellectual setting. Such views are reminiscent of Thomas Mann's contemporaneous essay "Notes of an Unpolitical Man." Thus Horney's basic unpolitical stance was also an expression of her time. She was not a feminist writer in our sense.

I have always viewed Karen Horney's early papers in the light of her courageous and intrepid liberation of her own thoughts from the constraints of Freud's libido theory, yet distinct from the themes of her mature writings. Seen in the context of her time, however, the papers reveal two interrelated themes of continuity among the intellectual currents of the period, her early theoretical concerns, and the structure of her new psychoanalytic theory. The two themes are self-realization and a new morality. As a central idea in all her work, the quest for self-realization most clearly reveals her roots in turn-of-the-century thought. The rhetoric about masculine and feminine principles was part of men's and women's quest to renew the spirit of being. This quest was invariably linked to a higher sense of morality, however differently conceived, and was most explicitly championed by the women writers. Not only is the question of morality raised by young Horney's discourse on monogamy and marriage, but it is central to "A Morality of Evolution," the introduction she wrote for her last book, *Neurosis Human Growth* (Horney, 1950). In that introduction, she clearly reiterates her ardent conviction that there is a moral dimension to the forces responsible for mental health or neurosis. She mentions the evil of the forces that hinder the realization of one's inherent potential.

I have tried to convey some of the flavor of the epoch that had a formative influence on Karen Horney. She lived in an era that saw the old world crumble and was eager to renew itself and venture in new directions. An unfailing instinct put her in the right place at the right time, and her undaunted spirit of search and creation was deeply congenial to major currents in her time. Setting her writings on feminine psychology amid the passions of the early 20th century does what history always does: it deepens understanding and connects her with her past, but also with the quests we pursue in living with our own past.

REFERENCES

Allan, J. (1973). *Wittgenstein's Vienna.* New York: Simon & Schuster.

Bachofen, J. (1964). *Myth, Religion and Mother Right.* Princeton, NJ: Princeton University Press.

Evans, R. (1976). *The Feminist Movement in Germany 1894–1933.* London: Sage Publications.

Green, M. (1974). *The Richthofen Sisters.* New York: Norton.

Horney, K. (1950). *Neurosis and Human Growth.* New York: Norton.

Horney, K. (1967–1973). *Feminine Psychology,* H. Kelman et al. (Eds.). New York: Norton.

Horney, K. (1980). *The Adolescent Diaries of Karen Horney.* New York: Basic Books.

Key, E. (1909). *The Century of the Child.* New York: Putnam.

Key, E. (1911). *On Love and Marriage.* New York: Putnam.

Simmel, G. (1984). *On Women, Sexuality and Love.* New Haven: Yale University Press.

Weininger, O. (1906). *Sex and Character.* London: Heinemann. (Originally published in the German language in 1903.)

3

Discussion of the Papers by Susan Quinn and Marianne Horney Eckardt

DOUGLAS H. INGRAM, M.D.

The papers by Susan Quinn and Marianne Horney Eckardt seek to discover those influences that accounted for Karen Horney's brilliant contributions to psychoanalytic theory. Marianne Horney Eckardt explores influences in the prominent thinkers and writers of her mother's era, whereas Susan Quinn tries to comprehend the personal motivations and immediate familial influences that contributed to Horney's successful efforts.

Of interest is that Eckardt avoids invoking the influences of more timeless thinkers. We need to turn to Rendon (1991), for example, if we wish to appreciate the threads of Hegelian thought in Horney's perspective. Shortly, I will argue that Nietzschian influences can be found in her work. Eckardt is more down-to-earth. She shows how the common ideas that circulated in the newspapers and in popular books provided the determinative intellectual ambience for Horney. Eckardt looks to the many whose fame is limited to their immediate audience, names all but lost to succeeding generations. In their work, she seems to suggest, we will find the true Weltanschauung from which still more influential thinkers may spring.

Eckardt singles out attitudes oppressing women in 19th-century Prussia as the prime cultural backdrop for Karen Horney's intellectual development. Masculine and feminine were used to designate the "two poles": reason, science, and authoritarianism versus sentiment, imagination, and the erotic. She notes how the journalist and satirist Karl Kraus—who presumably Karen Horney read—represented the rebellious spirit that developed in turn-of-the-century Germany, laying the groundwork for an attack on authoritarianism. That attack would emerge full-blown after World War I in what the historian Paul Johnson (1983) would call the start of the Modern Era.

Kraus, for his part, was influenced by Otto Weininger, who separated the masculine and feminine ideals, respectively, as the constructive and destructive, Aryan and Jewish. But Kraus, although accepting the distinction between masculine and feminine, argued that the feminine principle is the source of all that is inspirational and creative. "The feminine fantasy fertilizes the masculine reason and gives it direction." This allied with the ideas of Otto Gross for whom eroticism was the great force for life. These notions, together with the rediscovery of Bachofen's vision of society as based on a matriarchal order, provided an alternative to patriarchal attitudes that dominated Western culture during Horney's formative intellectual period.

It is to Gross that Eckardt traces Horney's later ideas of self-realization, psychic conflict, and the imposition of cultural factors on the growing individual. Of interest is that Eckardt is careful to avoid assertions that Horney was influenced by one person or another. Is she presuming influences that may or may not have mattered? Does she recall her mother reading certain books or periodicals, or hearing conversations in which so-and-so is praised, or damned? We are disappointed that we need to speculate in this way, that from the daughter we have mere hints about possible intellectual influences—not homey reminiscences.

Eckardt emphasizes that these new intellectual attitudes that men were embracing in their rebellion against patriarchy concerned male and female "principles." This had nothing to do with women as women. Men talking about women is still not women talking about women. Nevertheless, such discourse sets the stage for women to become active on their own behalf. Ellen Key, according to Eckardt, was outstanding in establishing and popularizing feminist concern. Again, we are implicitly asked to presume that she was a signal influence on the thinking of Karen Horney. The other main feminist influence on Horney, we are led to believe, was Helen Stoecker. Helen Stoecker's feminism was derived from Nietzsche's call to freedom from the bondage of tyrannical ideas.

Earlier I indicated that Horney's work has been traced to the influence of Hegel; now I wish to follow Eckardt's lead and raise the possibility that another significant philosophical background figure influencing Horney was Nietzsche. The Nietzschian perspective is most recently affirmed, at least in one aspect, in the school of thought known as deconstruction. It seems most useful to back into Nietzsche through a brief examination of deconstruction.

Deconstruction has as its goal the close analysis of rhetorical devices used by philosophers and other thinkers who wish to persuade their audience of some central tenet. It tends to challenge presumed authority, and—as with Nietzsche's work—provides a philosophical legitimacy to challenging established authority. This is the kind of tool that Horney would need. Out of her disaffection with Freud's phallocentric, patriarchical model, Horney sought to move the premise of psychoanalysis from biology to sociology, from absolutism to cultural relativism. Horney shifted to the view that culture determines in the most profound ways what we regard as healthy or sick. Horney's later theory is consistent with the inference that metaphors comprise the structures of language that predominate in any given culture and, hence, that contribute to a consensual vision of every facet of reality.

For example, in criticizing Freud, she criticizes the basic rhetorical device that was so persuasive to Freud's own culture, namely, the mechanistic-energistic model. Horney would argue, or I will argue on her behalf, that the "damming up of libido" was so attractive because it drew on this metaphor. Decades later, this same objection would be applied by Derrida, the founder of deconstruction. Derrida, like Nietzsche—and Horney, to an extent—is skeptical of all claims to truth. Nietzsche "anticipates the style and strategy of Derrida's writing to a point where the two seem often engaged in a kind of uncanny reciprocal exchange. . . . Nietzsche often seems to spell out in advance the program and systematic ruses of deconstruction, adopting the same attitude of skeptical rigour . . ." (Norris, 1982, p. 57).

Nietzsche emphasizes that thought is caught up with language, which in turn is caught up with metaphors. For Nietzsche, truth was a "'mobile marching army of metaphors, metonymies, and anthropomorphisms . . . truths are illusions of which one has forgotten that they *are* illusions'" (Norris, 1982, p. 58). And, writes Norris, "This bottomless relativity of meaning, and the ways in which philosophers have disguised or occluded their ruling metaphors, are the point of departure for Derrida's writing like Nietzsche's before him" (p. 58).

For both Nietzsche and Derrida, science is a discourse that arises from the equation, set forth by the Greeks, between truth and logic. They depart from logic and order, from Levi-Strauss and the structuralists, and we might add, from Freud, preferring instead an

> "innocence of becoming . . . a world of signs without fault, without truth, and without origin which is offered to an active interpretation" [Norris, 1982, citing Derrida, p. 60] . . . Truth is simply the honorific title assumed by an argument which has got the upper hand—and kept it—in this war of competing persuasions. . . . Thinking is always and inseparably bound to the rhetorical devices that support it. (Norris, 1982, p. 61.)

Horney would not go so far. Horney's relativism is, itself, relative. After all, she leaps to the faith that people are essentially constructive and that there is in each a person a "real self." She regarded her psychoanalytic model as based on an optimistic view of humanity. In these assertions, arguably the weakest aspect of her psychoanalytic theory from a purely intellectual standpoint, she recedes from rigorous skepticism.

The Weimar Republic's Berlin was the center for creativity in nearly all areas of endeavor. The Berlin Psychoanalytic Institute was, we could say, "modern," whereas the Institute in Vienna was embedded in premodern traditions. In Vienna, what was moral was unquestioned. In Berlin, morality was anything but certain. Ethical issues ramified art and science.

For Horney, mental health and illness possessed a moral component. Eckardt brings attention to the influences on Horney that informed this view. To the modern reader, the moral note Horney sounds in this connection may seem quaint. But this reflects our falling prey to a reign of positivism, with its dismissive scorn of ethical considerations. In essence, positivism holds that if you can't measure it, it isn't real knowledge. The epistemological basis for Freud's psychoanalysis is at one with this proposition. The Freudian position regards the psyche from a distance, studies it, and propounds presumably provable formulae that are ubiquitously applicable. The success of positivism has been a function of technological advances and the consequent creation of capital and awesome weaponry. The horrors of a positivism stripped of humanistic considerations became evident after the fall of the Third Reich and the horrors of Hiroshima and Nagasaki. The need to integrate ethics and science was amply discussed although, in fact, very little real gain occurred. The "two cultures" described by C. P. Snow remained separated, and do so to this day. In Weimar's Berlin, as in Horney's later writings, the issue of morality matters in what was regarded as a medical theory and therapy.

Nowadays, the contemporary struggle within psychoanalysis most akin to the question of whether ethical concerns are relevant to psychoanalytic thinking resides in the question, Is psychoanalysis scientific or hermeneutic (Ingram, 1992; Strenger, 1991)? Are we concerned with how what occurred developmentally caused a person to think, feel, and behave in a certain way? Or are we concerned with the structures of meaning that determine who one is? The Horneyan model tends to the latter, insisting on the primacy of the question, Who is the person now over who was the person earlier? In this, too, Horney's position is distinctly contemporary.

Horney, as noted earlier, relied at least indirectly on a Nietzschian perspective to overthrow the absolute reliance on biology as the basis for psychoanalysis. For Freud, psychoanalysis was very much a science; however, for Horney (1987) the question of whether it is a science or an art is not so clear. I wonder if Horney would be distressed with Grunbaum (1984), who invokes Popper's refutability criterion as determinative of what is true science. I wonder if she would worry if we are now less certain and have more humility that our interpretations—indeed, our entire enterprise—are regarded as lacking the imprimatur of a natural science. I wonder if she would be concerned with the challenges of Spence, who underlines that our interpretive hypotheses cannot claim historical accuracy:

> Freud made us aware of the persuasive power of a coherent narrative—in particular, of the way in which an aptly chosen reconstruction can fill the gap between two apparently unrelated events and, in the process, make sense out of nonsense. There seems no doubt but that a well-constructed story possesses a kind of narrative truth that is real and immediate and carries an important significance for the process of therapeutic change. (Spence, 1982, p. 21)

If we do require a sense that psychoanalysis is a science, we are better served by joining with the therapy process researchers (Dahl et al., 1988) and investigators of therapy outcome (Epstein & Vlok, 1981; Hine et al., 1982; Parloff, 1982). What can be made scientific, perhaps, is the study of what we do and of what happens, even if the scientific foundation—that we have from Freud—is in doubt.

The archeological model that Freud followed sought to uncover repressed memories and their associated affects. The hermeneutical model, however, seeks to impose a cogent narrative sequence on what is remembered in order to provide a sense of mastery over what is otherwise bewildering to the patient. This is a model that accurately describes the quality of emphasis that Horney brought to psychoanalytic technique, as we observe in her *Final Lectures* (1987). As alternatives to the archeological model, Spence, for example, offers as the basis for successful interpretation that it be aesthetic—that interpretation be coherent as well as pleasing as an experience—or, as yet another alternative, that interpretation be pragmatic. This reverberates with existential psychoanalytic views which were embraced by several of Horney's followers in the 1950s and 1960s.

Nevertheless, this in no way means that Horney's psychoanalytic ideas are devoid of concerns for development of the child. On the contrary, Horney emphasized the importance of understanding early development in order to better appreciate the patient who appears in our consultation room (Ingram, 1984; Lerner, 1983, 1985; Paul, 1984).

In closing this portion of my discussion, I believe Karen Horney would have applauded Eckardt's effort: it is a perspective that is both culturalist and humanist.

Susan Quinn finds Karen Horney to be an "important thinker." This is not universally shared. Quinn supports this contention by noting that Horney's paper on negative therapeutic reaction anticipated Anna Freud's *Ego and the Mechanisms of Defense*, citing Rapaport as her source. Likewise, Horney emphasized the significance of narcissism before its significance was well-recognized. Quinn persuasively demonstrates the extent to which Horney anticipated Kohut in this regard, an argument developed by van den Daele (1981), Danielian (1988), and Paul (1985, 1989).

Still, the most important contributions that Horney made were in feminine psychology. Quinn's summary of Horney's growing disaffection with Freud's phallocentrism is elegant. Her condensation of Horney's arguments is delightful, witty, and altogether persuasive. Quinn notes that Horney increasingly turned to social realities to explain the "flight from womanhood," abandoning the presumed biological basis for the plight of women—penis envy.

Quinn points out that Horney's significant writings were incorporated into the classical school of psychoanalysis without attribution. Perhaps it deserves to be pointed out, as well, that in her own writings, Horney makes little reference to others. To Horney scholars, as well as to the casual reader of Horney's work, the variety of rich new ideas that spring from the pages of her books, unreferenced, is utterly striking. She seems to have digested great and minor influences, made them her own, and then forgot the sources of these influences. Or, possibly, she just couldn't be bothered. Perhaps the intensity and vitality that Quinn describes rendered Horney impatient with what, for her, were intellectual niceties.

As a result, Horney appears to be the starting point for a certain kind of intellectual current. Of course, we know from Susan Quinn's estimable biography that Horney was very much involved with others in discussions of all kinds. I believe that Horney's failure to adequately reference other thinkers whose ideas she incorporated weakened her legitimacy as a scholar and served to undervalue scholarly pursuit by her followers.

Perhaps, though, we cannot have it both ways. It may be this same intensity, this independence of spirit, this longing to experience what is new—traits that run counter to patient, careful scholarship—that emboldened her to privately rebel against her father's authority and, later, against all authority. At the same time, Quinn speculates, Horney longed for faith, "'firm as a rock'" and that this longing may have reflected a desire to be close with her father.

Karen Horney's intellectual and creative energies were fired up by loss or rejection, according to Quinn. Out of her introspection, mobilized by psychic pain, she sought to understand herself and the commonalities she shared with all humanity. In this, as well as in other efforts of Quinn to understand the personality of Horney, we may well judge that the fabric of causal relation is too loosely woven. Quinn acknowledges as much. Still, it is fun to follow Quinn's thinking. What are the origins of Horney's originality? Of the originality in each of us? Quinn summarizes her own ideas in connection with Horney: intensity, intelligence, the tendency to question authority, the capacity to imagine fantastic possibilities, creative introspection as a response to loss, a sense of life's possibilities, persistence, and a mother's support and encouragement.

In the history of ideas, what makes an "important thinker" is not that ideas were good, or that ideas anticipated the ideas of others, and certainly not that the ideas of others were adequately cited and referenced. Instead, the criterion for being an important thinker is the effective influence of one's ideas. Ingram and Lerner (1992) hint at the possibility that Horney's position may have contributed to the rise of object relations theory. They argue that Horney, like the British school of object relations, departed from the traditional Freudian line, arriving at a point of view similar in many respects.

> [Horney's] objections were important and resonated with many in the psychoanalytic movement (Sayers, 1991). After she departed The New York Psychoanalytic Institute, she needed to develop a point of view which was comprehensive and enlightened, an alternative to the psychoanalytic model to which she and others objected. Horney elaborated an orientation that is compelling and useful to this day. Still, it deserves to be said that parallel forces within the main currents of psychoanalysis redressed some of these same grievances that irritated Horney, evolving theoretical perspectives that are now encompassed as object relations theory. It would not be correct to regard Horney as a forerunner of object relations, nor to attempt some metatheoretical fusion of her ideas with those of other object relations theorists. Her work stands solidly as it is. Yet as psychoanalysts working in a contemporary environment, we are served through an appreciation of how much her work and that of other object relations thinkers draw together, and at times even touch.

I wish to conclude these remarks by noting an irony in these outstanding papers by Eckardt and Quinn. We glimpse the person of Horney through someone who never knew her; we explore the intellectual influences on Horney with someone who knew her very well, her daughter. No, we will not accuse the biographer of vaulting arrogance for speculating, for interpreting the deep motivational structure of Karen Horney's creative spirit. That's her job, we believe, more or less. We take what she offers with interest and pleasure—and with a grain of salt. At the same time, we respect and honor the humility of the daughter who avoids speaking of the person, the mother she knew. That is a matter between them, a matter profoundly intimate and private. In the end, we appreciate that the mother of that daughter is not the Karen Horney we are entitled to know.

REFERENCES

Dahl, H. et al. (Eds.). (1988). *Psychoanalytic Process Research Strategies.* Heidelberg: Springer.

Danielian, J. (1988). Karen Horney and Heinz Kohut: Theory and repeat of history. *American Journal of Psychoanalysis, 48,* 6–25.

Epstein, N. B., & Vlok, L. A. (1981). Research on the results of psychotherapy: A summary of evidence. *American Journal of Psychiatry, 138,* 1027–1034.

Grunbaum, A. (1984). *The Foundations of Psychoanalysis: A Philosophical Critique.* Berkeley, CA: University of California Press.

Hine, F. et al. (1982). Effectiveness of psychotherapy: Problems of research on complex phenomena. *American Journal of Psychiatry, 139,* 204–207.

Horney, K. (1987). *Final Lectures,* D. Ingram (Ed.). New York: Norton.

Ingram, D. (1984). Discussion of "Horneyan Developmental Psychoanalytic Theory," by Dr. Henry Paul. *American Journal of Psychoanalysis, 44,* 97–102.

Ingram, D. (1992, January 23). *Fable, skepticism and metaphor as interpretive adjuncts.* Presented at the Association for the Advancement of Psychoanalysis.

Ingram, D., & Lerner, J. (1992). Horney theory: An object relations theory. *American Journal of Psychoanalysis,* 52, 37–44.

Johnson, P. (1983). *Modern Times: The World from the Twenties to the Eighties.* New York: Harper and Row.

Lerner, J. (1983). Horney theory and mother/child impact on early childhood. *American Journal of Psychoanalysis, 43,* 149–157.

Lerner, J. (1985). Wholeness, alienation from self, and the schizoid problem. *American Journal of Psychoanalysis, 45,* 251–258.

Norris, C. (1982). *Deconstruction: Theory and Practice.* New York: Routledge.

Parloff, M. (1982). Psychotherapy research evidence and reimbursement decisions: Bambi meets Godzilla. *American Journal of Psychiatry, 139,* 718–727.

Paul, H. A. (1984). Horneyan developmental psychoanalytic theory and its application to the treatment of the young. *American Journal of Psychoanalysis, 44,* 59–73.

Paul, H. A. (1985). Current psychoanalytic paradigm controversy: A Horneyan perspective, *American Journal of Psychoanalysis, 45*, 221–234.

Paul, H. A. (1989). Karen Horney's theory of self. In D. W. Detrick & S. P. Detrick (Eds.), *Self Psychology.* Hillsdale, NJ: Analytic Press.

Quinn, S. (1987). *A Mind of Her Own: The Life of Karen Horney.* New York: Summit Books.

Rendon, M. (1991). Hegel and Horney. *American Journal of Psychoanalysis, 51*, 285–299.

Sayers, J. (1991). *Mothering Psychoanalysis.* London: Hamish Hamilton.

Spence, D. P. (1982). *Narrative Truth and Historical Truth: Meaning and Interpretation in Psychoanalysis.* New York: Norton.

Strenger, C. (1991). *Between Hermenutics and Science: An Essay on the Epistemology of Psychoanalysis.* Madison, CT: International Universities Press.

van den Daele, L. (1981). The self-psychologies of Heinz Kohut and Karen Horney: A comparative examination. *American Journal of Psychoanalysis, 41*, 327–337.

4

The Myth of the New Impotence

Update for the 1990s

HELEN SINGER KAPLAN, M.D., Ph.D.

One of Horney's most important contributions was her recognition, early on, of the male bias in psychoanalysis. Horney was appalled by this and felt that it was incumbent on her to correct this blind spot. She realized that psychology had been until that time mostly worked at from the side of men, and it seemed to her to be the given task for women psychologists (or at least she thought it to be hers) to work toward a fuller understanding of specifically female trends and attitudes in life (Horney, 1967).

We now know that this conceptual heminopsia limited the theoretical validity as well as the therapeutic effectiveness of psychoanalysis, but in the male-oriented culture of that time when there was simply no awareness that a gender bias existed, this was an immensely important insight.

However, I will *not* speak today from a feminine perspective. That would be just as counterproductive and as inimical to good science as the exclusively masculine bias was in the past. Thanks in no small measure to Horney's insights, today there is no longer room for any gender bias or gender blindness in medicine or in mental health. The time has come for therapists and analysts and physicians to adopt a humanistic perspective, in recognition that we are a two-gender species; it is simply not possible to fully understand human behavior or to treat psychological problems effectively unless we comprehend and appreciate, without being judgmental, the similarities as well as the differences in the sexualities, psyches, bodies, brains, and acculturation of men and women.

This is especially true in my field, sex and marital therapy, which deals (at least in the case of heterosexuals) with problems in the relationship between men and women. Therapists who work with these problems are seriously handicapped unless they are attuned to and embrace both the male and the female view.

But it is not easy to eradicate all traces of gender bias in one's work. Masters and Johnson, who recognized the hazards of gender blindness for conducting sex therapy, were pessimistic about the ability of male or female therapists to truly understand the sexual experience of the other gender. In an attempt to solve this problem, they devised the male-female or dual-sex therapy team method, whereby two therapists, a male and a female, attend all the therapy sessions with both sexual partners.

Cotherapists are rarely used today. But the elimination of gender bias remains a paramount issue in our field. Thus we make a great effort in our program (the Human Sexuality Program at the New York Hospital–Cornell Medical Center) to train male and female therapists to familiarize themselves and to empathize with the sexual experiences of both genders, so that all our therapists can work effectively and comfortably with either male or female sexual problems. Moreover, since unconscious gender bias gives rise to destructive countertransferences and boundary violations in male and female clinicians, we do our best to raise our consciousness to gender-specific issues on a continuing basis, so that we do not undermine our work by acting out of these.

IS THE SEXUALLY LIBERATED WOMAN DESTRUCTIVE TO MALE SEXUALITY?

From such a "gender-free" or, better yet, dual-gender perspective, I would now like to examine the question of how the recent sexual liberation of women has affected male sexuality. This question first came up in 1972, when Ginsberg, Frosch, and Shapiro published an article in the *Archives of General Psychiatry* entitled, "The New Impotence." This paper generated an enormous amount of interest and controversy at the time and raised issues that are still very much alive today.

The authors presented case vignettes of four young impotent men and postulated that the women's seeking and expecting orgastic release, and also the fact that virginity was becoming largely irrelevant, were critical causal factors in these cases, and they suggested that this pathogenetic scenario was a widespread phenomenon. Frosch and his co-authors, Ginsberg and Shapiro concluded that the effect of increased sexual freedom of women on their male partners has resulted in an increase of complaints of impotence among younger men (Ginsberg et al., 1972).

At first my colleagues and I did not pay much attention to the article. We did not believe it, because it seemed obvious that the four sexually anxious, frightened young men upon which the authors based their thesis would have been dysfunctional in any cultural setting, with any lover, and that their current partners' sexual freedom had little or nothing to do with their impotence.*

Furthermore, the notion that sexually responsive women make men impotent was entirely at odds with our modern understanding of human sexuality. This was based on the outmoded sexist view, which makes caricatures of men and of women by depicting sex as something a man does *to* a woman (and if she doesn't hold still, he can't do it right).

However, the media had a field day. This modest article gave rise to an amazing journalistic eruption: a flood of newspaper, magazine,

*It is of interest that one of these men *recovered* his potency because of the kindness and support of his liberated partner.

and television pieces appeared in addition to articles and panels in medical journals—all declaring that psychiatrists had determined that the new liberated women's striving for orgastic equality was frightening men and causing a worldwide epidemic of impotence.

Was this myth or fact? Was it true that there was an increase of psychogenic impotence among younger men? And if so, were the sexual expectations of newly liberated women the cause?

Absurd as this seemed, with all the publicity, these questions could no longer be ignored. Therefore, in 1977, in preparation for a talk for the American Academy of Psychoanalysis meetings in Toronto, I considered these questions and concluded that the "new impotence" was a myth (Kaplan, 1977). My conclusion was based on two lines of evidence. One, I conducted an informal survey of major sexual problem clinics in the country, including Masters and Johnson's, Harold Lief's, our own, and others. The results were consistent: all the clinics I contacted did indeed show a significant increase of patient referrals; however, in none of these programs was this confined to men. There was an equal increase in the number of women who were complaining of sexual problems (but no one seemed worried about an epidemic of the "new frigidity").

It was the consensus of my colleagues that the increase in the number of men and women who were seeking help for their sexual dysfunctions could be attributed for the most part to the fact that people were beginning to feel more entitled to good sex, were becoming less embarrassed about complaining to their physicians about their sexual problems, and, most of all, because the public had become aware of the new effective sex therapy techniques with their promise of rapid cures. In other words, there was no real evidence of an epidemic.

Second, our clinical experience did not corroborate the notion that sexually liberated women were making men impotent. The partners of the impotent men whom we were then treating in our program—albeit they were mostly married, and not the single men described in the article—rarely exhibited the characteristics one would expect to find in sexually liberated women. To the contrary, it seemed to me on the basis of the relatively small number of cases we had seen at that time that a significant proportion of the wives of the impotent men we were seeing were anything but sexually liberated; they were more likely to be sexually inhibited and highly traditional in their sexual attitudes.

SEX IN THE 1990s

Some 20 years have passed since that time. Social conditions have changed once again, and we have learned a great deal more about impotence and its treatment.

From this perspective, I must now add that although no worldwide epidemic of impotence has materialized, the authors of "The New Impotence" paper were not entirely wrong. They astutely perceived that the changing social conditions were creating and/or exposing some sexual difficulties for men—as well as women, as the authors conceded in a later version of the paper (Frosch, Ginsberg, & Shapiro, 1979)—that we had not seen before. This was a valid observation. Unfortunately, however, the authors, all male, all with classical psychoanalytic training, looked at this exclusively from a masculine perspective. Thus they saw only half the picture, and not surprisingly, they arrived at some erroneous conclusions. In other words, Ginsberg, Frosch, and Shapiro were right in their observation that people were experiencing new types of sexual complaints, but they were entirely wrong about the role women played in this.

THE WINDOW

Between the pill in the 1950s and AIDS in the 1980s, there was a window of sexual opportunity and open sexuality that was unparalleled in the Western world for the last 2,000 years. Not since the Dyonesian orgies of ancient Rome had there been this much sexual licence. Casual sex was the mode. Extramarital sex was on the increase. Swinging clubs sprang up in the suburbs, and establishments that provided arenas for orgies, such as Sandstone in California's Topanga Canyon and Plato's Retreat in New York, in the Hotel Ansonia on West 72nd Street, were doing a land-office business. This was the brief moment in time when we had stopped worrying about unwanted pregnancy and we were not yet afraid of dying of AIDS.

The 1960s and 1970s were a time when you *could*, and in fact in certain circles *were expected to*, have sex with relative strangers on a casual basis. Thus in the 1970s it was quite usual for a single woman to go out on a blind date, and if there was nothing really awful about him, she would invite him to her apartment after dinner and they would make love. This was simply a part of the modern way of getting to know each other. If she didn't sleep with him by the second date, there was something wrong. Either he would suspect her of being "frigid" or he would conclude that she didn't like him. In either case, chances were that if one didn't have sex pretty fast, or if it wasn't good, one would never hear from that person again.

The sexual revolution was wonderfully liberating sexually and emotionally, and many people had the best time of their lives. However, this also created tremendous performance pressures. In those years many patients, both men and women, would come into my office and complain. My male patients would tell me, "I have taken her out three times and I have not yet tried to make love to her. . . . I'm afraid if I don't the next time, she will think that I'm gay or impotent, and I'm afraid that she's going to tell all her girlfriends. I couldn't stand the humiliation. But I'm scared, what if I can't have an erection?"

Or from recently divorced, middle-aged women, I would hear, "I have not dated for 15 years; I'm completely out of practice. It's a new world out there. All my friends are sleeping with their dates. But I'm scared to death. What if I don't have an orgasm? What if I don't lubricate? What if he wants oral sex? I have no idea how to do that—they won't take me out again. I'll never find another man. Help!"

Thus in the 1960s and 1970s there was increasing pressure on men and women, especially on those who were single, to perform sexually with new partners before they had a chance to become comfortable or intimate with each other. Many people, especially those who were older, who grew up imbued with the old antisexual attitudes, could not handle this pressure and got into trouble.

Again, in justice to the authors of "The New Impotence" paper, there are good scientific reasons to believe that this increased performance pressure had a more profoundly destructive effect on the male sexual response than it did on the female. Of course, women also felt pressured and used and traumatized emotionally. However, there are significant *biological* differences in the male and the female sexual response cycle, and from a purely physical point of view, women can handle sexual pressure better than men.

CURRENT CONCEPTS OF IMPOTENCE

To clarify the above point, let me say a few words about current concepts of psychogenic impotence.

Twenty years ago, when this controversy began, impotence was still considered a very serious condition, because we did not yet understand the biological or physiological causes of impotence; treatment was so poor that the majority of men who developed erection problems were faced with a lifetime of sexual disability.

In the past two decades, since the scientific study of sex became increasingly legitimate, the situation has improved dramatically. A panoply of laboratory investigations throughout the world have finally given us an accurate picture of the physiological mechanisms of erections and of the pathophysiology of impotence, as well as effective new medical treatments for potency disorders. Progress in the psychological aspects of the field have been equally impressive. The extensive clinical experience and data that accumulated in the 1970s and 1980s have clarified the psychopathogenesis of psychogenic impotence and have led to dramatic improvements in sex therapy to the point where the majority of cases can be treated successfully.

Performance Anxiety

In the past we believed that impotence was always the product of significant unconscious conflict which had its roots in painful childhood experiences. According to Freudian theory, these centered around unresolved oedipal conflicts, and impotence was seen as a defense against castration anxiety (Fenichel, 1945). Later it was recognized that men's "dread of women," that is, the fear of rejection by a lover, and the consequent narcissistic injury were also a potential cause of male sexual dysfunction (Horney, 1967). Culturally induced guilt about sexual pleasure and marital problems were also added to the deeper psychological issues that could give rise to potency problems (Masters & Johnson, 1970; Kaplan, 1974; Kaplan, 1979).

Now we know that although such deeper issues can play a role in some cases, by far the most common operating cause of psychogenic impotence, which can be seen in almost every case, is the patient's anxiety about his ability to perform sexually (Masters & Johnson, 1970).

A self-reinforcing cycle of performance-anxiety impotence, when this occurs in otherwise well-functioning men, is often the sole and only cause of erectile failure. However, in more complex cases, performance anxiety is only the tip of the iceberg of the patient's underlying unconscious intrapsychic and/or marital conflicts.

The Pathophysiology of Psychogenic Impotence

An erection is produced by a high blood pressure system in the penis. When a man becomes excited, certain reflexes cause the penile arteries to dilate, thus increasing the inflow of blood into the phallus. At the same time, reflex relaxation of certain smooth muscles in the corpora cavernosa acts like a tourniquet, which traps the blood at a high pressure against the tough envelope of fascia that encases the penis. This "hydraulic" mechanism is responsible for the rigidity of the penile erection. However, if a man should have an anxious thought while he is making love, for example, "I wonder if I'll be able to keep this erection," a physiological process is triggered that reverses the erectile mechanism. For an anxious thought is not a pure cognitive, CNS event. The experience of anxiety is always accompanied by the immediate release of *adrenaline* and *noradrenaline* into the circulation. These substances, which reach the penis almost instantly, cause the arteries to constrict, thus decreasing the inflow. Even more important, in response to noradrenaline, the smooth muscles of the cavernosa constrict, with the result that the "tourniquet" is released and the erection collapses

(Kaplan, 1974; Kaplan, 1979; Kaplan, 1989; Lue & Tanagno, 1987; Wagner & Kaplan, 1993).

Fear, or rather the adrenergic surge that accompanies fear or anxiety, also inhibits vaginal arousal, but in the female the effect is not as visible nor as incapacitating. Female excitement is also produced by reflexive vasocongestion of the genitalia (Wagner & Levin, 1987; Wagner & Levin, 1989). This produces a diffuse swelling of the genitalia and a transudate that lubricates the vagina. However, females do not have a complex erectile mechanism; although a woman may temporarily stop lubricating as the adrenaline surge hits her genitalia, this is usually quite temporary and still leaves her capable of having intercourse (Kaplan, 1974; Kaplan, 1987; Krane, Goldstein, & De Tajada, 1989).

Therefore, *in retrospect*, the new sexual complaints of men that Ginsberg, Frosch, and Shapiro astutely observed were *not* caused by sexually liberated women who wanted "orgastic equality." These difficulties were created by the destructive effects of sexual performance pressure that escalated dramatically in the 1970s. Although this affected both men and women, the effects were more visible and more devastating in males.

THE NEW MONOGAMY

The window between the pill and AIDS is now closed. We are no longer sleeping so quickly with strangers. Single people now get to know each other pretty well before going to bed, because they want to make sure that a new lover is not HIV-positive, and for the same reason, married folks now think twice before having affairs.

I have said that the sexual revolution is not dead and that the 1990s is the decade of "hot monogamy": now that we have gotten a taste of sexual freedom, we will never want to go back to boring, mechanical, guilt-ridden sex. We feel entitled to enjoy our orgasms and our erotic fantasies, and we want this on a regular basis. But it is becoming increasingly "in" to confine this good sex to *one* partner, and the terrible pressure to perform with strangers, before one is comfortable and before one is intimate, has now diminished considerably.

From this new perspective and with our increased scientific understanding of the causes and the treatment of impotence, it is now possible to reexamine the effects of the sexually liberated woman on male potency; I am very happy to report that the original hypothesis that had been based on the preliminary clinical observations in 1977, that is, that the new sexually liberated woman is *not* impotentogenic, has been supported by the extensive clinical experience that has been accumulated since that time.

First, it is clear that the partner's behavior and attitude *can* be extremely important for male sexual functioning, although this is not true in all cases. Some neurotic impotent men cannot function with any partner, no matter how attractive or accommodating she is. The sexual dysfunctions of these men are reflections of their deeper intrapsychic conflicts about sex, love, and women. In such cases the partner's sexual behavior and appearance are largely immaterial in the pathogenesis of the symptom of impotence and its treatment.

However, in many cases psychogenic impotence is partner-specific. Such men function well with some partners, but with those who mobilize their performance anxiety, they experience erectile dysfunctions.

HOW TO MAKE A MAN IMPOTENT

What kinds of women provoke anxiety in their lovers? Do men really experience more performance anxiety and impotence with sexually liberated women than they do with old-fashioned partners?

Since 1975 we have had the opportunity to evaluate over 5,000 patients and couples with sexual complaints, and we have treated approximately one half of these. Our observations of dysfunctional couples have clarified what sorts of partner behaviors and characteristics provoke impotence in men, and these clinical studies do *not* bear this out. More specifically, we have found the following three partner variables are consistently associated with performance-anxiety impotence: *insufficient desire*, *hostility*, and *inadequate sexual behavior*.

1. Lack of Sexual Desire or Attraction

Sexual attraction, or desire for the partner, is an important element of good sex—for men and for women—and a partner's lack of sex appeal can create problems.

Some men consider themselves impotent when they cannot manage to have an erection with an unappealing partner. However, this is not really impotence. This is a reflection of the sexist myth, which is based on an adolescent male macho ideal, that a "real" man is supposed to have sex with any willing female. However, it is completely unrealistic for a person to expect to enjoy love-making or to function well sexually in the absence of sexual desire. In fact, repeated attempts to have intercourse just because a woman is available, and without lust or desire can trigger a cycle of chronic performance-anxiety impotence.

The human sexual response cycle consists of three physiologically discrete, but temporarily and experientially overlapping and synchronous phases: desire, excitement (erection), and orgasm (ejaculation). On a biological level, sexual desire reflects the activation of the sex centers of the brain, and emotionally this lends pleasure and passion to the sexual experience. It is physically possible for a man to have erections, to penetrate, and to ejaculate in the absence of desire, but this tends to be an empty, mechanical experience, which yields little pleasure (Kaplan, 1993). Moreover, if this is repeated too often, the man is likely to develop a sexual aversion and secondary erectile difficulties. Incidentally, similar considerations apply to women who engage in sex with men who do not attract them. They too are apt to become aversive and sexually dysfunctional.

There are many reasons why a man feels no desire for his partner. Some are realistic: sometimes the partner of the impotent man is really not his sexual ideal or fantasy. In other cases the woman goes out of her way to make herself unappealing. She may do this by neglecting her hygiene and/or appearance. It is not surprising if a man develops sexual problems if his wife always wears curlers and a smelly old bathrobe around the house. Such behavior is indicative of the wife's sexual difficulties or of problems in the couple's relationship. But this has nothing to do with women's sexual liberation, for *it is not politically incorrect for a modern, liberated woman to be an attractive, loving, and skillful sexual partner!*

More often than not a man's sexual desire is blocked by his own emotional conflicts. Some neurotic men turn every lover into their mothers, while others simply cannot meld emotional closeness and erotic passion for the same woman, no matter how loving and attractive she is.

But whatever the underlying reason—his neurosis, her neurosis, or reality—if a man attempts to make love when he lacks desire, he is likely to develop trouble attaining and maintaining his erections.

2. Hostility and Rejection

A partner's *hostility* can make it difficult for a man to function, even though he finds her attractive, and even when he feels intense desire.

It goes without saying that hostility and rejection are inimicable to good sex, and there is no doubt that rejection of and anger toward the partner are major causes of impotence. This is true for women as well as men. An angry person, man or woman, who hurts, withholds, and undermines is a poor sexual partner, and lovers of such hostile persons frequently have problems functioning. In fact, couples who are engaged in violent struggles with each other are such poor candidates for sex therapy that we often have to work on improving their relationships and defusing their anger at each other prior to commencing sex therapy.

However, who says that sexually liberated women are so angry? I am not aware of any evidence that women with sexually liberal attitudes, and women who enjoy sex, are more hostile to men than those with traditional values. I feel that the suggestion that sexually liberated women are angry and vengeful and expressing their penis envy by making castrating sexual demands on men is insulting as well as unfounded.

3. Inadequate Sexual Behavior

Inadequate sexual behavior is perhaps the most important partner characteristic that is associated with male dysfunction. But it is a woman's *sexual inhibitions*, rather than her pleasure in sex, that are likely to contribute to the development of impotence in her partner.

A woman who is sexually anxious and does not enjoy love-making, who is unresponsive, and who has trouble lubricating and reaching orgasm is a poor sexual partner. For a lover's sexual arousal is an aphrodisiac for most men, and there is nothing as reassuring to a man than to see that he is giving his lover pleasure. Conversely, a partner's unresponsiveness can be threatening and mobilize crippling performance anxiety, especially in rejection-sensitive men.

Sexually inhibited women typically avoid sex, overtly or covertly, and they seldom initiate sexual contact. It is this *rejection*, rather than the expression of sexual desire by the liberated woman, which tends to raise sexual anxiety and the loss of sexual confidence in their partners.

Partners of impotent men are often *poor communicators*. Sexually inhibited women do not know what they need sexually, and they do not feel entitled to equal consideration in bed. For these reasons, they tend to have difficulty expressing their sexual needs clearly. This lack of feedback leaves the man anxious and uncertain about "how he is doing" sexually.

Unreasonable sexual demands are probably the single most important source of performance-anxiety impotence. I do NOT mean by this the so-called demands for "orgastic release and sexual pleasure" of the liberated woman. There is no pressure involved if a woman likes to have orgasms, as long as she doesn't object if this is provided by her partner's hand, his mouth, or a vibrator, or for that matter by herself. But real pressure is created by women who rely on their partner's erect penis to validate their sense of worth.

Women who were brought up with traditional, sexist values often measure their sense of worth primarily by the response they receive from men. To such women, especially if they are also emotionally fragile, the husband's erect penis comes to be equated with their own adequacy. Conversely, these women are deeply threatened by their partner's erectile failure and take this as a painful personal rejection, regardless of physical realities. I have seen women weep in despair because they believe that if their husbands "really loved them," they would be able to have erections, despite the medical proof of a physical problem in the form of a diagnosis of diabetes and a flat NPT (nocturnal penile tumescence) record.

Tremendous performance pressure is created for the man who knows that his wife's emotional well-being depends on the firmness and staying power of his erections, and he knows that she will be devastated or furious at him if he should fail to "perform."

Moreover, such traditional and inflexible partners typically refuse to accept clitoral stimulation and insist on lengthy vaginal penetration as their only mode of satisfaction. They also tend to object to erotica, often on the grounds that this is perverse. Such limitations put additional performance pressures on their partners, especially as they age.

I do not mean to imply that these men's impotence is the partners' wish or their "fault." These women are poor sexual partners but only because they themselves are victims of their antisexual and sexist upbringing.

The following case vignette illustrates the role of a wife's traditional sexual behavior in the pathogenesis of her husband's impotence.

Case 1: Unliberated Wife—Liberated Lover

The patient was a 50-year-old successful surgeon married to his wife, age 45, for 20 years. The chief complaint was recurring and chronic impotence.

Mrs. A was a stunningly beautiful woman. She was the product of a highly traditional sexist, antisexual upbringing, and she had never masturbated, nor had sexual fantasies, and her husband had been her first and only sexual partner. She felt that intercourse was the only "right" way to make love, and she objected to his stimulating her orally, which was his greatest fantasy. She was passive in bed, and she expected him to take full responsibility for love-making. In addition, although she was occasionally orgastic, she did not often enjoy and generally avoided love-making. When she did consent, it was clearly out of a sense of duty. Yet she felt devastated when he couldn't function, and if her husband lost his erection, she would often weep into her pillow.

The immediate cause of A's impotence was his performance anxiety, which was heightened by his wife's inflexible sexual attitudes and her unreasonable expectations. On a deeper level, this patient was pathologically rejection-sensitive, and his overconcern about pleasing and performing for his wife fueled his performance anxiety.

This couple responded with a temporary improvement of their sexual relationship to a brief course of sex therapy, which focused on reducing the husband's performance anxiety and improving the couple's communications. However, they were both resistant to exploring their deeper problems; not surprisingly, the patient's impotence recurred one year after the end of treatment.

I saw this patient again five years later. He came to see me because his wife had instituted divorce proceedings. He was devastated and attributed this to his impotence.

This time in therapy he was willing to explore his problems with women in depth. At the same time that we were tracing the childhood roots of his sexual conflicts in the therapy sessions, I also encouraged him to practice masturbating while watching erotic videotapes or fantasizing. The objective of these "homework assignments" was to restore this patient's sexual confidence, which had been so badly eroded by his disastrous relationship with his wife, that A considered himself impotent and incapable of a normal relationship.

He made rapid progress and soon met a sexually liberated woman who was two years older than his wife. She was not as attractive, but she was Mrs. A's virtual opposite in terms of her sexual behavior. She appreciated his interest in oral sex and she was multiply orgastic with this form of stimulation. Moreover, she often initiated lovemaking, she adored spending as much time in bed with him as possible, and she assured him that he was a wonderful lover.

The patient now has no sexual problems. During a recent follow-up visit, he told me that he is experiencing the best sex of his life, and the couple are planning to marry.

Do I mean to suggest that impotent men should leave their traditional wives and seek partners who are freer sexually? Of course not. I cited this case to illustrate the point that sexually liberated behavior on the part of women does *not* cause impotence in men; it can actually enhance male sexual functioning.

It is of course much more usual in sex therapy to work with both partners and to help an inhibited woman overcome her sexual blocks and to expand her sexual horizons, for herself as much as for her partner. I wish I had been able to do this with Mrs. A.

The following case is more typical.

Case 2. The Liberation of a Traditional Wife

Mr. and Mrs. C, both in their late 50s, married for 27 years, came to see me about Mr. C's impotence, which had its onset more than a year before. Prior to that, the Cs made love once a week without any problems.

Similar to the previous case, the husband's performance anxiety was the immediate cause of his impotence, and the wife's unliberated sexual attitude was a factor in maintaining the symptom. However, although Mrs. C, like Mrs. A, was a poor sexual partner because of her traditional sexual behavior, she never said "no" to her husband, and she did not avoid sex.

The patient's impotence began when he was in the midst of a threatening business crisis. His partner had embezzled money from the business, and the IRS was after Mr. C to pay taxes on money that he did not have.

During this stressful time C had experienced some episodes of erectile failure, which had quickly escalated into a chronic cycle of performance-anxiety impotence.

Mrs. C loved her husband and wished to help him. However, both came from highly traditional, religious backgrounds which had not equipped them to cope with this problem.

They had fallen into a stereotyped sexual routine. Mr. C was always in charge, intercourse was their only form of sexual activity, the lights were always out, they always used the missionary position, and they always had sex on Friday night. Oral sex and erotica were out of the question and the couple had never spoken to each other about sex. This unliberated sexual behavior had been okay until the onset of the husband's impotence. But now he needed more flexibility and stimulation from his partner, as well as more open communication, in order to break the cycle of performance-anxiety impotence.

This case had a happy ending. Mrs. C was basically a healthy woman who had been brought up in a loving family. Her sexual inhibitions were mainly cultural and not neurotic in origin. This woman had felt left out of the sexual revolution and wanted to be liberated, but she didn't know how to go about this. She had even had a fleeting thought of starting an affair with the gardener, but she panicked at the mere thought. However, she was not at all resistant to learning about oral sex and erotica and about having orgasms with a vibrator. She rapidly became a much more active and flexible partner. The Cs now often have morning sex, she loves getting on top, and sometimes they watch an erotic videotape together. Not surprisingly, her husband has recovered his potency.

TREATING THE MALE AND FEMALE COMPONENT IN SEXUAL THERAPY

I do not want to overstate the case. Although it is certainly true that we do not treat the symptomatic partner in isolation, but consider the *sexual system*, or the *couple's relationship*,* as our "patient" and as the focus of our interventions, I am highlighting here the role of the partner in the pathogenesis and treatment of partner-specific impotence, primarily to detail just why and how the liberated woman is facilitative rather than destructive to male potency.

However, I don't want to leave the impression that we send our impotent patients home and then work with their wives to make them more accommodating sexual partners. It is certainly *not* our policy to exclude the symptomatic partner, be this the man or the woman.

Again, the most common immediate cause of psychogenic impotence, and the *final common pathway* by which a variety of

---

*Masters and Johnson (1970), in an extreme expression of their systems view of sexual inadequacy, considered the "marital unit" their patient.

stressors impinge on the sexual response, is sexual-performance anxiety. Therefore, *the reduction of performance anxiety* is a major aim of all therapies for impotence, psychoanalysis, and marital therapy as well as sex therapy. To take this one step further, if this can be accomplished, the man's functioning will improve even if he is left with some unresolved residual deeper or concurrent intrapsychic or marital problems. Conversely, if the treatment does not succeed in reducing the patient's performance anxiety, he will remain impotent no matter what other gains he makes, no matter how valid the insights are that he attains in analysis, and no matter how much his relationship with his partner improves in marital therapy.

In sex therapy we use highly sophisticated and effective methods to diminish performance anxiety. These consist of an integrated combination of therapeutic "homework assignments," which deemphasize performance and emphasize instead the mutual exchange of sensuous pleasure and sexual parity between the partners. These therapeutic "exercises" often preclude intercourse, while the couple touch each other gently, communicate their feelings to each other, and explore each other's genitalia and fantasies. In general, they strive to become more aware of their own and their partner's sexual sensations, instead of concerning themselves with the hardness or the staying power of the man's erections. These strategic interventions are coupled with psychodynamically oriented exploration of the man's deeper resistances and defenses against sexual adequacy, love, and intimacy (Kaplan, 1974, 1979, 1986).

However, when the partner's unreasonable sexual expectations about her husband's sexual capabilities, or her own sexual anxieties, are material in heightening his performance anxiety, the focus of treatment shifts to her, and the goal of therapy then comes to include the modification of her anxiety-provoking sexual behavior. This often entails granting the woman "permission" to enjoy her sexuality and helping her to become orgastic, for her own and her partner's benefit.

CONCLUSION

Fears have been voiced that male potency will be a casualty of the sexual revolution, which has brought greater sexual freedom to women. However, there is no scientific evidence that this is true. On the contrary, everything we know about male and female sexuality and about potency and impotence tells us that men and women are equal beneficiaries of the social forces that are finally freeing women to experience their natural biological heritage of sexual pleasure.

I would certainly like to hear from, and have a dialogue with, my male colleagues about these issues.

REFERENCES

Fenichel, O. (1945). *The Psychoanalytic Theory of Neurosis.* New York: Norton.

Frosch, W. A., Ginsberg, W. A., & Shapiro, T. (1979). Social factors in symptom choice. In T. B. Karasu & C. W. Socarides (Eds.). *On Sexuality: Psychoanalytic Observations.* New York: International Universities Press.

Ginsberg, W. A., Frosch, W. A., & Shapiro, T. (1972). The new impotence, *Archives of General Psychiatry, 26*(3), 218–220.

Horney, K. (1967). The dread of women. In H. Kelman et al. (Eds.), *Feminine Psychology.* New York: Norton.

Kaplan, H. S. (1974). *The New Sex Therapy.* New York: Brunner/Mazel.

Kaplan, H. S. (1977, May). *The Myth of the New Impotence.* Presented at the American Academy of Psychoanalysis, Toronto.

Kaplan, H. S. (1979). *Disorders of Sexual Desire.* New York: Brunner/Mazel.

Kaplan, H. S. (1987). *Sexual Aversion, Sexual Phobias, and Panic Disorders.* New York: Brunner/Mazel.

Kaplan, H. S. (1989). The concept of presbyrectia. *International Journal of Impotence Research, 1.*

Krane, R. J., Goldstein, I., De Tajada, I. S. (1989). Medical progress: Impotence. *New England Journal of Medicine, 321*(24), 1648–1657.

Lue, T., Tanagno, E. (1987). Physiology of erection and pharmacological management of impotence. *Journal of Urology, 137*, 829–836.

Masters, W., & Johnson, V. (1970). *Human Sexual Inadequacy.* Boston: Little, Brown.

Wagner, G. & Kaplan, H. S. (1993). *The New Injection Treatment for Impotence: Medical and Psychological Aspects.* New York: Brunner/Mazel.

Wagner, G., & Levin, R. J. (1978). Vaginal fluid. In E. S. E. Hafez & N. Evans (Eds.), *The Human Vagina.* Amsterdam: Elsevier.

Wagner, G., & Levin, R. J. (1984). Human vaginal and sexual arousal. *Fertility and Sterility, 41*, 389–394.

5

Discussion of the Paper by Helen Singer Kaplan

HAROLD I. LIEF, M.D.

Contemporary Gender Relations and Male Sexual Functioning

It is altogether fitting that a meeting devoted to the subject of female psychology is in honor of Karen Horney. For it was Horney who presented and wrote the initial dissenting views about female psychology, setting herself in opposition to Freud, a courageous stance for an ambitious woman in the 1920s.

Horney offered a very different perspective of female development to psychoanalytic students. She described processes of identification very different from Freud's and spoke of vaginal awareness in children, while she was aware of the continuing role of the clitoris in adult sexual life. Yet, as her biographer, Susan Quinn, points out, she still was so influenced by Freud's views concerning vaginal orgasm that she never overcame her guilt engendered by her greater enjoyment of clitoral stimulation than by coitus. Horney wrote that "I would not for the world admit that this sort of pleasure gives me more satisfaction than the *nor-*

mal sort" (Quinn, 1987, p. 163). Even though she had to a large extent emancipated herself from the phallocentric views of Freud, it was difficult for her to make this ultimate break with Freud's libido theory.

Psychoanalysts who believe in penis envy and the vaginal transfer theory will view male-female relations very differently from those who eschew those ideas. I have singled out for discussion these two key Freudian notions. They are key elements in the theory of psychosexual development and are highly significant in the way clinicians approach patients. These beliefs, positively or negatively held, have a profound impact on the way men and women regard each other, and hence affect relationships and their artistic expression in literature and art.

PENIS ENVY

Horney challenged the assumption that male (and female as well) children automatically and inevitably develop castration fears because of the absence of the penis in females. Envy of female children toward males was deemed by Freud to be a way of warding off the threat of castration. Horney pointed out that men can and do envy women over their child-bearing capacity, and even if envy of one gender regarding the attributes of the other are present, it is, in all likelihood, the consequence of later developments in the life of the child, strongly influenced by cultural pressures. Although anatomical differences ("anatomy is destiny") and their perception may be significant in individual cases, these differences usually become important only if reinforced by such cultural influences as the differential societal power exerted by men and women.

Even at the level of early developmental influences on the child, Horney posited that the early identification of male and female children with the mother is likely to be a more important influence on subsequent behavior than the awareness of genital differences. The boy has the more difficult task of disidentifying with his first love object, his mother, and transferring his identification to his father. It is perhaps for this reason that almost all the paraphilliacs and the majority of those who are arrested, who kill others or themselves, are men.

In this regard, it is interesting to witness the enthusiasm for books like Robert Bly's (1992) *Iron John: A Book About Men.* Bly sees men as being unmanned by the failure of identification of the male child with an *Iron John* or the "Iron Hans" of Grimm's Fairy Tale. The failure, in Bly's view, is the failure of father-son bonding. Whether male strength can be achieved without recourse to male patriarchy or sexist behavior is the issue.

There is abundant evidence today of genetic, even anatomical CNS differences between the sexes, as in the hypothalamus, leading to cognitive differences in males and females. These differences and even the hormonal influences of fetal life can be facilitated or inhibited by the culture acting upon the family as mediator.

"Anatomy is destiny" is a simplistic notion; we are more complex creatures than that, and Horney struck an early blow for pluralism and complexity in human development.

VAGINAL TRANSFER THEORY

Freud believed that the clitoris was the female counterpart of the penis—a view challenged on anatomic grounds in recent years by Josephine Lowndes Sevely (1987) in her book *Eve's Secrets.* The smaller clitoris was an indication of female inferiority. This is how he put it: "The little girl's clitoris behaves at first just like a penis, but by comparing herself with a boy playfellow the child perceives that she has come off short and takes this . . . as a reason for feeling inferior" (Freud, 1961/1924, p. 173). Freud believed that the adult woman has the task of transferring the seat of sexual excitation from the clitoris to the vagina, and if the female fails to make this transfer, it is evidence of a childhood fixation and an indicator of neurosis or immaturity.

Sex therapists and researchers are in agreement that the majority of women do not regularly have a coital orgasm, but they do orgasm with clitoral stimulation. Even those who report orgasm during intercourse often augment their erotic response by "clitoral assistance" (simultaneous stimulation of the clitoris). Actually, the vagina is not insensitive as many have believed for a long time; there are areas, especially in the anterior wall of the vagina and the area between the top junction of the labia minora and the urethra, that are especially sensitive.

Orgasm is a coordinated reflex response of the clitoris and vagina and probably the urethra and even the uterus as well. The bottom line is that there is hardly a sharp differentiation between a "clitoral" orgasm and a "vaginal" orgasm.

In psychoanalytic practice, for decades, women who did not transfer their excitation from clitoris to vagina, who did not have a so-called vaginal orgasm (a transfer that makes no sense to us now) were labeled as neurotic, or at best immature.

In this regard, I recall a supervisory session with A. A. Brill, Freud's translator, in early 1947. He was discussing with a small group of supervisees a patient he had recently seen for depression. The patient had been to a previous analyst who had suggested that the patient was immature because she had never had a coital orgasm. The patient had sought help originally because of a depression, which intensified after the analyst's appraisal of her character. She had the good sense to leave her first analyst and to seek help from Dr. Brill. Brill pointed out to his patient, and now to us, just how ridiculous this notion was. After the teaching session had concluded, in view of the importance of the issue, I asked Brill why he did not publish his ideas, correcting the widely held notion about the vaginal transfer theory. He looked at me with astonishment, almost as if I had slapped him in the face. To put into print a criticism of "The Master" was clearly unthinkable.

The nature of female sexual response and the woman's general attitude toward relations with men are significant items in the examination of impotence. This connection lies behind the idea that female pursuit of sexual pleasure puts additional burdens on the male, whose performance anxiety is increased by the need to please his partner to the point of erectile failure. Kaplan was asked to examine this issue; I agree with her conclusions, namely, "Our clinical experience did not corroborate the notion that sexually liberated women were making men impotent." If anything, the reverse is true—a sexually responsive woman at home with her body and confident of her responsivity is apt to help a frightened or inexperienced man overcome his anxieties. I refer you to the play *Tea and Sympathy* as an example of this theme.

Again, as Kaplan says, it is the woman who is inadequately responsive that puts a greater burden on male performance. If the man feels that his wife or partner is insufficiently responsive because of his inadequacies as a lover, the pressure mounts to overcome her nonresponsiveness. It is in this setting that impotence frequently occurs. A rather dramatic example of this was presented by Phillip Sarrel some years ago (Sarrel, 1982). He treated a group of more than 30 couples; all of the husbands were impotent, and the women postmenopausal. He put the women on steroid replacement therapy but did not treat the men. Nevertheless, in all but one case, after the women became more responsive and more interested in sex, the impotence was reversed.

If a man believes that his wife's sexual satisfaction is his responsibility primarily, he may feel extraordinary pressure to perform, which results in erectile failure. An example of this is a physician whom I saw many years ago. He had left his wife for a younger woman and they had moved to another part of the country in order to avoid community censure. However, he was guilty about having removed her from her friends and family and felt that it was up to him to ensure her happiness. Although he had had no trouble with erectile failure while he was courting her, the pressure on him to perform and to please her became stressful. The pressure to perform increased to the point where he became impotent. He and his bride came to see me. As a consequence of this single consultation, in which his wife heard of his need to satisfy her, which was followed by her reassurance about her commitment to him, the impotence disappeared.

We sex therapists have a cliché we try to convey to our patients. We tell them, "You are not responsible for your partner's orgasm." Like most clichés, it is only partly true. The idea behind this statement is to get the partner to communicate what he or she needs or prefers to become sexually aroused. For we are and should be responsive to our partner's sexual desires, preferences, patterns, timing, setting, and so on, and ultimately to our partner's responsivity. The partner's pleasure is often the best aphrodisiac. The natural and healthy response is to feel good if our partner demonstrates pleasure. Women who are responsive rarely intimidate or threaten men unless they compare the man unfavorably to present or past lovers.

At the beginning of my commentary I discussed penis envy. One school of thought has been that envious women retaliate by "castrating" men. Actually, more women tend to be afraid of a large penis than those who get turned on by "Long Dong Silver." At least this is true in clinical practice. It is men who really have penis envy. Among men, perceptions of having a small penis is so frequent that it has to be inquired into in taking a history with every male who shows evidence of sexual anxiety. I even have seen a handful of men who exhibited the "Koro Syndrome," thought to occur only in the Orient. These are men who believe that their penises have shrunken to the point of being useless for sex. One of my patients was a physician who caught his wife in bed with another man. Overnight his penis began to shrink, according to him, and he was so desperate that he became suicidal. Penis envy as *penis* envy, not as a symbolic representation of power (though it is that as well) is much more frequent in men than in women.

THE SEXUAL LIBERATION MOVEMENT IN THE 1960s AND 1970s

To a great extent, striking changes in sexual permissiveness in the 1960s and 1970s was felt among college-educated people. The availability of the pill had a lot to do with it. There was an increase in premarital sexual activity and in the number of partners before marriage. The change in sexual behavior from previous decades occurred mainly among women. Some studies showed that women entering college in the mid-1970s had a higher percentage of coital activity than did male freshmen. Because of AIDS, the situation in the 1980s and 1990s is very different. The carefree, casual, and rapid bedding-down is disappearing. Yet, despite the fear of contracting a fatal illness, the rate of coitus among the unmarried has not changed appreciably. By the age of 19, 80 to 90 percent of teenagers have been coitally active. "Just say no" is like putting a Band-Aid on a cancer. It would be helpful if we could get teenagers to postpone their first coital activity from 15 to 18, so the slogan "Just say no for awhile" might fall on more receptive ears.

Kaplan is right when she says that women "can handle sexual pressure better than men" because their responsivity is much less apparent than a man's. It is questionable whether they handled the *social* pressure better than men during the decades of the 1960s and 1970s. After all, this was the group that was making the major change, and many women were in great conflict about switching from the old value system to the new one.

The change was not so dramatic for men. In our society, men are programmed from an early age to "score" with women. The emphasis is on proving one's manhood, not on attachment. Until very recently there was not even a focus on responsible sex. The new sexual permissiveness fed right into this macho orientation. Most men who had relatively little emotional baggage from their childhood or teen years found themselves capable of performing. On the other hand, those men with developmental disabilities who came upon this scene with sexual anxieties from their prior years had trouble living up to the social myth that Zilbergeld calls the "fantasy model of sex" in which the penis is "two feet long, hard as steel, and can go all night" (Zilbergeld, 1992, p. 30).

All too often it was better for the female if the male couldn't perform. Those men who could and did often had irresponsible or painful relationships with women, in which the women were often ultimately rejected and abandoned. Perhaps women could deal with this situation better sexually, but I have grave doubts whether they handled it better socially, given the cultural myths with which they had to contend. One might ask, which is worse, a broken penis or a broken heart?

There are many routes for the growth of feminism, but one of them was a reaction against the callous superficiality of male-female relations in those two decades. Although a search for a greater share of power, with the ultimate goal that of equality, was a dominant theme in feminist rhetoric, the basic wish, it seems to me, was a drive for increasing respect from men.

Although some women became more aggressive and acted more like the stereotypic male, looking for a "zipless fuck" (Jong, 1974), and were possibly "castrating" to their male partners, many more women were confused and uncertain about how to negotiate the changing social scene. This confusion and uncertainty created anxiety that had, in many instances, an inhibiting effect on female sexual functioning. Therapists were much more apt to see women with inhibited sexual functioning, especially inhibited sexual desire, than those disappointed because of frustrated desire.

MECHANISMS OF ERECTION AND ERECTILE DYSFUNCTION

Kaplan discusses performance anxiety and the effect of that anxiety on erectile capacity. When she discusses the mechanism of erection, she states it correctly: "the reflex relaxation of the smooth muscles of the corpora cavernosa acts like a tourniquet which traps the blood at a high pressure against the fascia of the penis. This mechanism is responsible for the rigidity of the penile erection." However, she then goes on to say that *anxiety* acting through the release of adrenaline and noradrenaline causes "the smooth muscles of the cavernosa to *relax*." She is right in the first instance and wrong in the second. Obviously, you can't have it both ways. Erection is caused by three processes:

1. Increased arterial inflow;
2. Decreased corporal resistance created by a *relaxation* of the smooth muscles of the cavernosa; and
3. Decreased venous return.

> The most plausible theory at this time is that the cavernous smooth muscles of the corpora, under neurological control and a constant state of contraction, relax. This lowers the vascular resistance of the corpora and results in a significant increase in blood flow to the penis. The dilated corporal spaces then cause passive occlusion of their venous drainage, allowing blood to pool in the corpora at systemic pressures, and thereby producing erection (Melman, 1992, p. 67).

In the flaccid state, the smooth muscles of the corpora have to be in a state of contraction. Anxiety maintains that state or returns the hemodynamic process to its original state, namely that of constant contraction. If this thinking is correct, the cholinergic system is largely responsible for the relaxation of the smooth muscles of the corpora and the sympathetic or adrenergic system for its contraction. The cholinergic or parasympathetic system seems to be largely responsible in both men and women for the physiologic processes, primarily vasocongestion, during a state of sexual excitation.

The physiologic system described above is even more complex because it has been demonstrated that stimulation of nonadrenergic/noncholinergic neurons produces relaxation of the corporal smooth muscle. Recently, it has been determined that nitric oxide is the mediator of this nonadrenergic/noncholinergic neurotransmission. At this point, it is at least suggestive that this additional pathway "may be involved physiologically in mediating penile erection" (Raifer, Aronson, Bush, et al., 1992, p. 94). The investigators of the effects of nitric oxide point out that this is the mechanism (release of nitric oxide) by which smooth muscle relaxation is obtained through the injection of Papaverine or Prostaglandin E1 when injected intracavernosally, causing tumescence.

Whatever the physiologic mechanisms, it is clear that Kaplan is right when she says that anxiety inhibits erection. The correction is that anxiety causes constriction of the smooth muscles of the corpora rather than relaxation. We also know that anger can do the same thing so, presumably, any emergency emotion can act that way, for example, guilt. Incidentally, a number of studies have pointed out that small amounts of anxiety increase sexual arousal and erectile capacity, at least in sexually functioning men, whereas moderate amounts interfere. These studies have been reviewed by Rosen and Beck (1988) who state, "moderate levels of anxiety . . . may diminish his awareness of affective and cognitive processes such as fantasies, which play a critical role in facilitating arousal" (p. 265).

The facilitation of arousal may induce premature ejaculation. Any male who can remember what his reactions were as a teenager trying to make out with his girlfriend in her parent's living room will attest to the differential effects of anxiety. If the young man thought her parents were coming in at any moment he might not have an erection at all, but if he thought they were due in 10 or 15 minutes and the anxiety was somewhat less, he was apt to have a premature ejaculation.

RELATIONSHIP FACTORS IN ERECTILE DYSFUNCTION

In other publications, Kaplan has separated the causative factors in sexual dysfunction into *immediate* and *long-range*. The most important among the immediate causes is performance anxiety; other factors such as expected emotional reactions of the partner may also contribute. Long-range causes were to be found in experiences in childhood and early adult years; also included are significant marital conflicts. Levine (1992) has made a helpful addition to our conceptualization of this by dividing these "spheres of causality" into three groups.

1. Performance anxiety in which the phase of time is the "here and now of lovemaking."
2. Antecedent life events—months to years, or "recent" history.
3. Developmental vulnerabilities—childhood/adolescence (remote history).

If we wish to retain Kaplan's words, we could speak of *immediate*, *intermediate*, and *long-range* causes.

Long-Range Causes (Developmental Vulnerabilities)

Levine (1992) lists gender identity problems, homoeroticism, paraphilia, abuse history, and diagnosable mental illness as among the developmental vulnerabilities that can cause primary and secondary erectile dysfunction (occurring after a period of normal functioning). It will take us too far afield to discuss these causes of erectile dysfunction and be a digression from our main concern with new concepts in feminine psychology. A discussion of women who are married to men with these developmental disabilities and how they adapt or cope in such relationships would justify a separate contribution, so I will confine my remarks to two examples that have a profound influence on male-female relationships.

Special Types of Developmental Disabilities There are two special types of developmental disabilities that deserve special attention. The first is the Madonna/Whore Complex. Many men find that their sexual interest wanes or disappears when there is a committed relationship. They discover this on the wedding night or shortly thereafter or even sometimes at the time of engagement. It may appear for the first time after the wife becomes pregnant or gives birth. These are men who retain their erotic interest in women to whom they have no commitment, especially if there is some degradation of the female, wherein the woman is perceived as being in a lower social class or status, a "bimbo," or even an out-and-out prostitute.

Usually, pornography has a great deal of interest to these men. They have not been able to fuse affection and excitement or love and lust. The most common reason for this is guilty fear over a less-than-conscious sexual interest in mother and a subsequent identification of wife with mother. These men usually lose sexual desire for their committed partner, but if they retain any, it is likely to result in erectile failure.

In rare instances, a male may find a female with a similar developmental disorder, leading to an unconsummated marriage.

> A couple were married for five years but had not had sex since their formal engagement. Eventually, they sought help after a lot of indecision. Neither one of them would initiate sex. Both sabotaged behavioral sex therapy and would refrain or otherwise interfere with the Sensate Focus Exercises. It was clear that there were substantial psychological problems that both had brought from their past.
>
> After a good deal of investigation, the husband finally disclosed that a much older brother had impregnated his sister, who was eight years older than the patient. This became a ter-

rible family secret. It made sex with any committed partner ("family member") guilt-ridden.

The wife, in the meantime, had been sexually abused by her father as a young adolescent. Although she, in the main, had resisted his advances, there was also an enormous attraction to her father, creating great guilt. Like her husband, she had been passionately interested in sex until their formal engagement and then found one excuse after the other to avoid sex. When they had tried on several occasions, the husband had been impotent.

A second developmental vulnerability stems from a violence misconception of sex. Freud labeled it a "sadistic misconception of coitus." Some men perceive sex as an aggressive act, because sex has been combined with violence in their childhood homes, either through sex abuse, parental quarreling, or a misperception of the sounds of coitus. This may lead to inhibition of desire or erectile failure, or, in some instances, to rape or rape/murder. There are many more men who are inhibited sexually by this misconception than those who act out in an aggressive manner. (More women than men have this concept because of real or fantasized life events, such as sex abuse, or rape, or harassment, leading to impairment of social and sexual functioning.)

Intermediate Causes (Antecedent Life Events)

Many antecedent events are significant factors in the causation of erectile failure. Vocational problems such as loss of a job is a highly significant one, since, in our culture, the man equates his potency with his effectiveness at work and his capacity as a lover; therefore, any work failure is apt to cause erectile dysfunction. However, I wish to concentrate on the area that Dr. Kaplan concentrates on, namely the relationship between men and women. She cites lack of *sexual attractiveness*, hostility and rejection, inadequate sexual behavior, and demanding sexual partners as some of the most important factors.

When a man tells me that he loses his erection because he has insufficient desire for his wife because she is too fat, I often find that the man himself is significantly overweight. He seems to be disavowing a part of himself that he dislikes and projecting that onto his wife. When a woman feels that she is not attractive, it can definitely inhibit her sexual desire and responsivity. I find this many times in postmenopausal women who are still yearning for their girlish figure lost after childbirth and years of inadequate exercise. This feeling of lack of attractiveness may cause a lot of rejection on the part of the woman. Her dislike for self turns to dislike of her husband and rejection of his advances. When this happens, one often finds a man having difficulty maintaining an erection. Once again, it is an example of a woman with inhibited sexuality rather than positive assertive sexuality who creates a problem in her partner.

Hostility and Rejection Hostility by itself may not provoke a man's erectile failure but rejection ultimately will. If rejection is combined with contempt, it is "castrating."

I can recall a woman who had a secret lover and needed to keep her husband impotent in order to justify her extramarital adventuring. As long as he couldn't "get it up," she had every reason in her mind to seek out a more competent lover. In such an instance, a man generally has a combination of anger toward his rejecting spouse as well as anxiety because of the excessive need to please her and possibly win her back. Either emergency emotion is capable of producing erectile failure. The combination of the two is lethal.

I do not regard such a "cheating" woman as "sexually liberated." Female adultery has been present at every age, and women with traditional beliefs are not immune to the temptations of extramarital sex. In my script, the truly liberated woman would have told her husband that she had found a lover who was more sexually desirable and then dealt with the consequences in an honest fashion. In the case I described, divorce followed anyway.

Inadequate Sexual Behavior I believe we agree that women who are sexually inhibited and poor sexual partners are much more apt to cause erectile failure in their partners than are those women who are sexually responsive. This fits in with the long-ago discovery by Masters and Johnson that if one partner in a couple presented for a sexual dysfunction, there was a 50 percent chance that the other partner was dysfunctional as well.

Demanding Sexual Partners I would like to emphasize Kaplan's point that women who believe that their personal worth is dependent on sexual intercourse, penis in the vagina, rather than some other source of release, tend to create a situation in which erectile failure is a distinct possibility. The woman who believes that the husband has to prove her lovability and attractiveness by inserting his penis in her vagina is putting excessive pressure on her partner. There are women who refuse to accept a penile prosthesis or the penile injection method or the vacuum pump method of overcoming erectile dysfunction because of its artificiality. In her view, if the man thought she was really attractive and desirable, he wouldn't have to have recourse to such devices.

CAN A SEXUALLY LIBERATED WOMAN CAUSE IMPOTENCE IN HER HUSBAND?

The bulk of the evidence is that it is the nonresponsive woman who is more apt to create erectile failure in her partner. However, it is possible that the "new woman" can cause the "new impotence." These cases are rare, but two examples do come to mind. In both cases there was a conflict, however, in the woman. She married a "weak" man in order to control or dominate him but then objected to his lack of strength in the sexual sphere.

> In one case, a man who had been brought up by his widowed mother and four maiden aunts in a small town in the South had no sexual trouble in his first marriage. After his wife died of cancer, he remarried. His second wife was a professional with a professional and not unpleasant assertive manner. In some fashion he was able to pick up her sexual fantasies, which had never been openly communicated. In her fantasies, she was made love to by real "macho" men, such as stevedores, truck drivers, construction workers, and so on.
>
> She married a journalist who led a very sedentary and quiet

life, quite unlike her fantasy male partner. Although this woman had been sexually active prior to marriage, she was not very responsive with her husband, and he responded to this nonresponsivity with erectile failure, so that even in this instance of a "liberated" woman, the woman falls into the nonresponsive category.

In another example, a married woman had a five-year intermittent relationship with a very masculine lover and increasingly could not conceal her contempt for her wimpy husband. Eventually, he lost his capacity for erection. If one examines this relationship, however, the wife's use of rejection and contempt were the decisive factors, not her sexual responsivity.

FINAL NOTES ON CONTEMPORARY MALE/FEMALE RELATIONS

In the 1990s both men and women will be looking for two things: commitment and intimacy. Women are looking to men who have a combination of strength and sensitivity, or, as one reporter said, a combination of John Wayne and Alan Alda. This is a tough recipe to fill and there will be many disappointments. Men are looking for women who have a combination of sexiness and nurturance. This also is a tough recipe to fill. If men have not achieved the capacity to combine lust and love, the woman's attempt to combine them in herself may prove fruitless. In the generation of AIDS people will be much more reluctant to dissolve ongoing relationships and are more apt to try to work out the nuances of conflicting identifications and needs. I see plenty of work for sex and marital therapists in the coming decades.

REFERENCES

Bly, R. (1992). *Iron John: A Book About Men.* New York: Vintage Books.

Freud, S. (1961). The dissolution of the Oedipus complex. In J. Strachey (Ed. and Trans.), *The Standard Edition of the Complete Psychological*

Works of Sigmund Freud (Vol. 19, p. 173). London: Hogarth Press. (Original work published 1924)

Jong, E. (1974). *Fear of Flying*. New York: Dutton.

Levine, S. B. (1992). Intrapsychic and interpersonal aspects of impotence: Psychogenic erectile dysfunction (pp. 198–225). In R. C. Rosen & S. R. Leiblum (Eds.), *Erectile Disorders, Assessment and Treatment*. New York: Guilford.

Melman, A. (1992). Neural and vascular control of erection (pp. 55–71). In R. C. Rosen & S. R. Leiblum (Eds.), *Erectile Disorders, Assessment and Treatment*. New York: Guilford.

Quinn, S. (1987). *A Mind of Her Own: The Life of Karen Horney*. New York: Summit Books.

Raifer, J., Aronson, W. J., Bush, P. A., et al. (1992). Nitric oxide as a mediator of relaxation of the corpus cavernosum in response to nonadrenergic noncholinergic neurotransmission. *New England Journal of Medicine, 326*, 90–94.

Rosen, R. C., & Beck, J. G. (1988). *Patterns of Sexual Arousal*. New York: Guilford.

Sarrel, P. M. (1982). Sex problems after menopause: A study of fifty married couples treated in a sex counseling program. *Maturitis*, Chapter 4.

Sevely, J. L. (1987). *Eve's Secrets: A New Theory of Female Sexuality*. New York: Random House.

Zilbergeld, B. (1992). The man behind the broken penis: Social and psychological determinants of erectile failure (pp. 27–51). In R. C. Rosen & S. R. Leiblum, (Eds.), *Erectile Disorders, Assessment and Treatment*. New York: Guilford.

6

Women's Psychological Development

Connections, Disconnections, and Violations*

JEAN BAKER MILLER, M.D.

In thinking about Karen Horney, I thought I would like especially to honor her boldness, the boldness and courage it took for her, as a woman, to pursue her observations—and to speak about them to the leaders of psychoanalysis, especially to *the* big leader, during a time when women's voices were almost never heard.

I know women—and men—who are afraid to do that today, who can't even begin to think in such terms. However, it is not just an individual's fear. I think it is important for us to think hard about the ways institutions create a climate that turns off people's questioning and creativity. Sometimes they do this in very gross and obvious ways, as they did to Karen Horney. Sometimes they do it in very insidious but pervasive ways, as they probably did to Karen Horney

*This is a revised version of a paper published in *Work in Progress, No. 33*, by the Stone Center Working Paper Series, Wellesley College, Wellesley, MA 02181.

also. It may be hard to believe that even now this kind of suppression of women's work is going on in many institutions.

Indeed, there is a danger that the vast outpouring of work by women of the last two decades may be covered over and lost. A few years ago, I heard Juliet Mitchell, who has been looking into such things, say that in Europe in the 1920s and 1930s the most prominent and hot topic of discussion in psychoanalytic circles was the psychology of women. And I believe Karen Horney's work on women started it all. Yet, when I began my training in psychiatry in the 1950s in the standard places, I heard nothing about it. The psychology of women—and Karen Horney's work—were all covered over.

Thus, I hope that through conferences, like this, and other ways we can continue to come together to discuss new ideas on the psychology of women—and their implications for the total human condition. In doing so, we will carry forward the best of the spirit of Karen Horney.

I'm particularly pleased to be honoring Karen Horney together with Carol Gilligan in this book. It seems that one way to think about all of the recent work on the psychology of women is to divide the work into two groups. One group of women have worked on modifying existent theories, such as Freudian, Jungian, object relations, and others. Other workers have begun by listening very closely to women and then finding that women's experience leads to the necessity for new assumptions—assumptions different from those that underlay prior theories. I think that the work of Carol Gilligan and her colleagues is that kind of work. I believe that her work and my own work emerge from a very similar basic approach. It is not surprising, then, that we find ourselves talking in similar ways.

This paper is part of an effort to lay a general base for understanding psychological problems that grow out of trying to listen to women's experiences. I'll begin by reviewing some of the Stone Center's work on the "centrality of the sense of connection in women's lives," and then try to suggest how psychological troubles—or what are called "pathologies"—follow from the disconnections and violations that women experience.

CONNECTIONS

We (at the Stone Center), along with Carol Gilligan, have suggested that if we study women's experience closely without attempting to force our observations into prior categories, we find that an inner sense of connection to others is a central organizing feature of women's development (Gilligan, 1982, 1987; Jordan, 1986, 1987; Miller, 1976, 1986; Surrey, 1984, 1987). I would summarize it briefly this way: women's sense of self and of worth tend to be grounded in the ability to make and maintain relationships (Miller, 1976). Most women find a sense of value and effectiveness if they experience all of their life activity as arising from a context of relationships and as leading on into a greater sense of connection rather than a sense of separation.

Once we take this observation seriously, however, we have to reexamine what we mean by *relationships.* What kinds of relationships exist or should exist? Again, if we stay close to women's lives, and if we examine the *kinds* of connections in which women have been functioning, we find that a large part of women's life activity can be described as "the active participation in the development of other people" (Miller, 1976), certainly that of children but also of adults. This activity has been characterized by such terms as "nurturing," "mothering," "satisfying others' needs," and the like. However, these words to not adequately describe the complex activity involved, that is, engaging with another person(s) in such a manner that you foster the psychological development of both (all) people involved in the interaction.

Another way to describe this activity is to say that traditionally women have used their powers to increase the powers of others, that is, to increase the other persons' resources and strengths in many dimensions—emotional, intellectual, and so on (Miller, 1982).

Almost all theorists agree that people develop by interaction with other people. No one develops in isolation. In these interactions, if women or men are not acting in ways that foster the others' development, they inevitably are doing the reverse, that is, participating in interactions in ways that do not further other people's development.

To talk of participating in psychological development is to talk about a form of activity that is essential for all societies. In general, this is essential activity that has been assigned to women. Thus, women have particular knowledge about it (but this knowledge has not entered into prior theories). From this knowledge, I believe we can begin to propose a form of development *within relationships* in which everyone interacts in ways that foster the psychological development of all of the people involved, that is, something we might call *mutual psychological development.*

Historically, our basic formative relationships have not been founded on the basis of mutuality. This condition has led to many complicated ramifications. For example, growth-fostering interactions have been going mainly in one direction: women have been fostering other people's growth. This is a societal situation, but our major theories reflect the societal situation. Criteria for maturity, for example, have not included characteristics such as the ability to engage in interactions that foster the development of all the people involved; nor do descriptions of development delineate how the child would "learn" to engage in such relationships. Instead, psychological theories, in general, have focused on a line of development that is cast in terms of a series of psychological separations from others.

Thus, as we have not had a societal situation based on the search for full mutuality, we have not had theories about the kinds of relationships that foster mutual development through childhood and adult life. Workers at the Stone Center have begun to sketch the outlines of such an approach. Surrey (1984) proposes three underlying processes: mutual engagement (I would prefer the word "interest" or "attention"), mutual empathy, and mutual empowerment. Jordan describes some of the characteristics of mutuality as relationships develop over time (1986) and suggests the redefinition of knowledge of self (and other) and of desire, which would follow from an "empathic-love mode" of development as contrasted with a "power-control" mode (1987). Kaplan (1984) suggests that the basic human motive—if we can speak of such a thing—can be better understood as the motive to *participate* in connections, rather than the need for "gratification" by others, a premise basic to prevalent developmental theories. Compare this outlook with Fairbairn, who stated that "the human being is basically object-seeking" (1952); however, he meant that the human being was seeking to obtain gratification from the "object."

Mutual Growth

As Surrey (1987) suggests, then, the goal of development is the increasing ability to build and enlarge mutually enhancing relationships. These are relationships that foster the continuing development of all the people involved in them. As the quality of the relationships grow, the individual grows. Each individual can develop a larger and more complex repertoire and can contribute to, and grow from, more complex relationships. The goal is not an increasing sense of separation but of enhanced connection—and, in turn, this connection leads to more growth.

Exactly how do connections lead to psychological development? And what do mutual engagement (or attention), mutual empathy, and mutual empowerment look like? I don't think that anyone has laid out a fully developed description yet, but we can begin with some proposals. To explain these complicated topics briefly, I'll use an example of an interchange between two adults. (This example is taken from an earlier working paper [Miller, 1986.]) The same basic features apply to children's development, but such an example would require a much longer discussion because of the different levels of ability at each age in childhood.

> A woman, Ann, has just heard from her friend and coworker, Emily, that Emily may have a serious disease. Ann is telling another friend, Beth, about this. Tears are in Ann's eyes and her voice sounds sad and fearful. Beth says, "Oh, how sad." Beth's voice and expression are sad and there is also some fear in them.
>
> Ann then says, "Yes, but I have this other awful feeling—like fear. Like I'm scared—as if it could happen to me." Beth replies, "Me, too. It is frightening to hear this. Maybe we all feel as if it's happening to us."

> This exchange goes on and Ann eventually says that she realizes that she had been feeling that "it wasn't right to feel afraid." She had felt it would be "selfish" to be afraid, as if feeling the fear meant that she was feeling and thinking about herself when she should be thinking only about Emily at this time. Both Ann and Beth talk further about their sadness, fear, and other feelings. As they continue, they both feel more in touch with what they suspect Emily may be feeling, and they come to feel more able to be with Emily in those feelings, although, of course, they don't know exactly what Emily is feeling.

To suggest a contrast, we can look at a different kind of interaction.

> Suppose Ann began this conversation with a different friend or a family member, or with her husband, Tom. I'll use the example of Tom. After Ann's first statement, with tears in her eyes and a sad and fearful voice, Tom says, "Well, it's a terrible thing. In the end, she'll have to do the best she can. She should get a second opinion. I hear the Sloan Clinic is very good on these kinds of cases. Have you called her back yet? Did you call my sister Helen about the birthday party she's trying to arrange for my mother next week? We should really do something about that if it's going to come off." As the conversation continues, Tom's greatest emotional interest seems to center on the birthday party, or what Ann should do about the party.
>
> Ann goes on with the conversation about the party because that seems to be Tom's emotional focus, and she tends to think automatically that he's right about what's important. She does this because she's trying to stay in connection with him. However, Ann now feels worse than she did before this interchange began. She dreads phoning Emily.

The first example may sound ordinary—many of us have thoughts, conversations, and feelings like this all the time, especially women. But I do not think it is ordinary in terms of its value.

And the valuable actions Ann and Beth demonstrate are not *ordinarily* recognized. I believe they contain the key features that make for psychological development in children and adults.

First, in regard to the process of psychological growth, I think it's apparent that the key processes are that *both* participants are responding empathically to each other. This is mutual empathy. Because they feel this empathic response, each is able to "take off" from this empathic base and add additional feelings and thoughts as they arise for her. These additions create the interaction, the flow. This mutually empathic interplay is created by both and builds new psychological experience—growth—for both.

The results of this process are that both people develop psychologically in at least five important ways. Both women feel an initial *connection* with the other, which gives them both a sense of increased "zest" or energy. This feeling has not been well described, but it is the feeling we have when we know that we have connected with another person. We also know the opposite feeling, the "down" sort of feeling when we know we have not connected. Second, both are able to be *active right in the relationship itself*, and they feel more empowered to act beyond the relationship—in this example with Emily. Ann and Beth both have more knowledge of self and other, a little more understanding about their thoughts and feelings; and these feelings and thoughts now further provide a stronger and more knowledgeable feeling-thinking base, which motivates action. Fourth, because these processes have occurred, both feel a greater sense of worth. Fifth, both desire *more connection* as a result. (The earlier paper provides more explanation about why and how both Ann and Beth experience these results, but I hope this summary conveys the general idea.)

In this interaction, it is not a question of giving or getting, nor helping or being helped, nor being depended upon or dependent. It is an interaction in which both people participate and enlarge and therefore want more of the same—and want the connections that make for such enlargement.

Each person has what I'll call for the moment "feeling-thoughts," that is, thoughts and their attendant feelings. Ann's feeling-thoughts are not identical to Beth's, but she can be empathic to Beth's feeling-thoughts. She is also able to receive Beth's feeling-thoughts and allow them to be different. Indeed, she *welcomes* and *enjoys* the different feeling-thoughts. She "feels" them as the necessary new factors that make both her and the relationship more than they were in the moments before.

DISCONNECTIONS

Now, I'd like to turn to disconnections—or the sense of disconnection that occurs when a child or adult is prevented from participating in mutually responsive and mutually enhancing relationships. Clearly, these disconnections occur when a child or adult is grossly abused or attacked, when the surrounding relational context is unresponsive to the child or adult's expression of her experience, or, as is usually the case, when both of these occur simultaneously. However, many minor disconnections occur all through childhood and adult life. They do not lead to serious trouble, especially if there are also many enlarging connections. Children and adults can withstand and even grow from these small disconnections.

I think the key factors making for growth when there is a threat of disconnection are the possibility that the child or adult can take action within the relationship to represent her experience and that the others in the relationship can respond to it in a way that leads back toward a reconnection.

To take a familiar kind of example, suppose a one-year-old child is playing along and then for some reason feels distressed and starts to scream and cry. For their own reasons, her parents can't deal with this well at the moment, and they respond with angry rebukes. Let us say that the child now feels startled and afraid, in addition to the distress she felt in the first place. She may also feel angry in reaction to her parents' anger and their lack of responsiveness to her. Most important, she now experiences a much more complex mixture of feelings, and she probably feels confused.

However, if the child *can turn* to her parents and then experience some acceptance of her distress and some responsiveness, she has been able to play a part in turning the interaction around. So have the parents.

The results of this interplay are many. Most important, as emphasized above, the child feels an increase in *her ability* to have an effect on the relationship between herself and others, that is, to build empowering connections. So, of course, do the parents. Several infant researchers recently have documented this ability—even in very young infants, for example, Stern (1985) and Gianino and Tronick (1985).

Both the child and the parents have learned a little more about their feelings. Obviously, this clarification occurs at a different level for the child than for the adults. Let us say, without spelling out the details, that all the participants have learned a little more about how the relationship can encompass fear, anger, and other feelings and how they can all move the relationship along *in the feelings* to a better sense of connection.

Serious Disconnection

To suggest a more serious disconnection, we can consider the example of Ann and Tom. Again, we could use a similar example with a child at each age in life. Obviously, I don't mean that one interaction like this leads to serious troubles, but the story of Ann and Tom can serve, too, to suggest that the processes that lead to troubles are not always so noticeable, especially if seen from only one point of view. They can occur in multiple daily disconnections extending over the course of life, as well as in more gross and obviously destructive situations.

Looking at Ann and Tom's interaction, I think we can see that these kinds of disconnections can lead to serious consequences if they continue *without a change in direction.* We can talk about the consequences in two dimensions: first, the immediate effects of this kind of interaction and, second, what an individual does about it over the course of time—and why.

In the immediate interaction, in addition to the initial fear and sadness Ann felt, she may now feel some shock and additional fear at Tom's response. She also feels angry now. She feels out of touch with Tom—or out of connection—and confused about how to get back into it.

For the sake of example, let us say that we know that this topic aroused sadness and fear in Tom, but he has not learned much about how to handle these feelings within connections with others. He becomes angry if someone threatens to evoke these feelings in him. (We could add that there are several possible reasons for Tom's responses. For example, he mentions his mother. She is getting older, is ill, and he may be concerned about her. Another possibility is that he becomes worried about Ann when he hears of an illness in Ann's friend.) Although Ann may sense Tom's feelings, she is not clear about them in the face of what Tom is expressing—and what he's not expressing.

Here again, Ann (and any child or adult) begins to experience not only bad feelings, but a confusion of feelings. Ann probably is picking up all of Tom's mixture of feelings, including his sadness and fear. But Tom is not saying he's sad or afraid. By contrast with the example of Ann and Beth, Tom and Ann's feelings and thoughts can't be "between them" or "with both of them"; so it feels to Ann as if they are all hers.

Like the child in the first example, she also feels angry now. First, she "picks up" Tom's anger. In addition, she becomes angry in response to Tom's actions. This anger becomes tied to and confused with the other feelings.

Ann is now in greater distress—a child would be in even more. Just because she feels in more distress, her basic reaction would be to want *even more* to try to connect with the other person(s). Suppose, again for the sake of example, she tries to express some of this to Tom. In response, he becomes only more angry and attacking, and then withdrawn—or withdrawn without overt anger and attack. Now Ann's mixture of confusing feelings and their intensity increase vastly. And a child's would escalate even more. Here, Ann has tried to change the course of the interaction but has been unable to do so.

To emphasize the point, Ann experiences a compounded reversal of the sense that her "feeling-thoughts" help to create a better connection—which would in turn lead to more action and empowerment. Instead she may begin to believe that something is deeply wrong with her important feelings if they lead to such troubles. And if her important feelings are so wrong and bad, she must be wrong and bad. For Ann, as for all of us, her feeling-thoughts *are her.* As

Janet Surrey has commented, Ann feels, "If there seems to be such a problem, I must be the problem" (personal communication, 1987). Ann feels the problem must be *in her.*

To add to Ann's tendency to believe that the problem is in her, she now feels angry but is confused about the anger. This kind of confused anger will augment her feeling that she is wrong and bad. Thus, Ann's initial feelings of sadness and fear mix with her confusion about anger. All of these feelings confuse Ann's sense of what happens when she tries to connect with others about important feelings.

To summarize Ann's immediate reactions to disconnection, they are the opposites—not simple opposites, but intensely confounded opposites—of the "good things" that flow from growth-enhancing, mutually empowering connections. That is, Ann feels less able to take action but, more than that, she feels that her actions, *based in her experience*, lead to great trouble. Here, it is important to stress the terrible sense that one's actions based in one's feelings are destructive. We can see that this kind of experience leads a person to clamp down on freely flowing, more spontaneous actions—to a person's creating her own imprisonment along with terrible suffering. Obviously, Ann feels a great decrease in her sense of worth, really a belief in her unworthiness. She has less knowledge about herself and about the other person(s), and more confusion. She experiences a decrease in "zest" or energy and a diminution of her sense of well-being. Most important, she feels that her actions, feelings, and thoughts lead to less connection with the important other person(s),—and not only less connection, but also a confusing sense of disconnection and isolation.

I want to call attention to this kind of disconnection. I believe that the most terrifying and destructive feeling that a person can experience is isolation. This is not the same as "being alone" in the more straightforward sense. It is feeling locked out of the possibility of human connection. This feeling of desperate isolation is usually accompanied by the feeling that you, yourself, are the reason for the exclusion. It is because of *who* you are. And, along with it, you usually feel helpless, powerless, unable to act to change the situation. People will do almost anything to escape this combination of condemned isolation and powerlessness. Here, I think I am talking about something close to Horney's idea of "basic anxiety." I would emphasize the context of disconnection.

Long-term Consequences

In the face of the terror of condemned isolation and powerlessness, Ann wishes even more to make connection with the people in her life, because she now experiences more threatening and complex "feeling-thoughts." She longs for connections with others to try to deal with these feeling-thoughts. This leads to the second area of consequences.

Before going on to that, I want to make a distinction between certain kinds of feelings. If we continue to talk about Ann, we can say that Ann now has an increasingly difficult and confused mixture of feeling-thoughts. For the sake of illustration, I've said that her initial feelings were sadness and fear. Although these are difficult feelings, they probably represent an inevitable response to what's really happening. They can be borne and borne best in connection with other people who can engage with them. Now, however, this original sadness and fear are combined with all of the other much more difficult feelings, and these are all mixed up with Ann's belief that she is bad to have all of these feeling-thoughts. Thus, she has moved from feeling sad and fearful to a much more complex, confused mixture of feelings. This is different. It is also a mixture of feelings that she never had to have in the first place. They are not necessary responses to the original event. They are responses to the forces operating within the relational context in which the event occurred.

Added to this picture is a most important point that I haven't developed here. For the sake of simplicity, I've used an initial event occurring outside of Ann and Tom's relationship, that is, Emily's illness, as an example in the development of the dynamics of disconnection. However, in the onset of serious troubles, it is usually the actions of family members, themselves, that lead to problems. Not friends of the family, but members of the family evoke the sadness, fear, or other feelings in the first place. And these same family members will have the most trouble allowing the child or adult to express her reactions to their actions. The adults who bring about serious disconnections and violations of the child (or other adults) also will have the most trouble engaging in growth-enhancing interactions about the results of their own behavior. All of us do this to varying degrees; but whenever one person has more power in a relationship, there is greater danger of harm because the less powerful person has much greater difficulty in altering the course of the interaction.

To return to the main thread, when children and adults feel the threat of condemned isolation, they try to make connection with those closest to them in any way that appears possible. This attempt leads to the next set of consequences, consequences that often proceed over a long time for many people throughout their development. That is, if a person cannot find ways to change the relationships available to her, she will take the only possible step: attempt to change the person possible to change—herself. Specifically, she tries to alter her internal image of herself and others, her internal image of the nature of the connections between herself and others. She must attempt this alteration alone, since the available relationships preclude doing it in interaction with others. In essence, the child or adult tries to construct some kind of an image of herself and others, and of the relationships between herself and others, which will allow her entry into relationships with the people available. This is a complicated process. In order to twist herself into a person acceptable in "unaccepting" relationships, she will have to *move away from and redefine* a large part of her experience—the parts of experience that she has determined are not allowed.

The attempt to alter her conception of relationships is complex and can take various forms. For simplicity, we can talk about the example of Ann and Tom, but we can think of this process occurring in children within a family, and occurring with added complexity because of the level of psychological ability at each of the younger ages. Ann could assume that the only way to find connection with Tom is to act on what she thinks he seems to desire. Thus, she tries to act on his wishes—or what she construes as his wishes—and she could be wrong about these. She has "learned" that only a bad person has feelings such as sadness, fear, anger, and the like, so she tries to become a person who never has such feelings. She has only good, pleasant, and positive feelings—such as wanting to love Tom and to do what Tom wants.

When events occur that would likely cause sadness, fear, anger, or any of the "unacceptable" feelings, she feels great upset but cannot be certain what she is experiencing—except that she shouldn't be feeling whatever she is feeling. It means she is bad.

It is important to emphasize that while there is initial confusion about many feelings in nonmutual relationships, certain feelings become especially prominent over time. One is fear (or anxiety). Ann has to become increasingly afraid of other people, because any other person is likely to evoke some of the "forbidden thoughts and feelings." Further, she has to become afraid of large portions of her own experience, because she inevitably will experience many feelings that threaten to disrupt narrowly constructed images of self and others. One particularly prominent feeling that threatens such disruption is anger. Anger certainly would threaten Ann's image of herself as a person who must have only good and loving feelings. Simultaneously, no one can undergo violations of her own experience and long-term threats to connection without serious anger (in addition to the common everyday causes for anger).

Over time, a large part of what Ann does and says does not arise from *her* experience within relationships. Her actions come from what she believes she must be in order to be allowed into connection with others. Thus, much of what she actually does in the world, often very worthy actions, do not connect fully with her own experience. To the extent that these thoughts, feelings, and actions are not originating from her perceptions and desires, nor connecting with her experience, they cannot build her image of herself as worthy. Moreover, they cannot alter the inner, increasingly walled-off portion of herself that consists of all the "bad" feelings and thoughts.

Here, I want to note one major paradox. In order to connect in the only relationships available, Ann will be keeping more and more of herself out of her relationships. She is maintaining relationships at the price of not representing her own experience in them. To this extent, she cannot be relating fully in the ways that lead to growth. Moreover, the parts of herself that she has excluded are unable to change from experience. Her continuous construction of a sense of self and others cannot benefit from the interchange within connections—precisely the source of clarity and knowledge needed for the development of an increasingly accurate image of self and others (as suggested in the illustration of Ann and Beth). Ann is constructing inner images of relational *possibilities—and impossibilities*—with less and less actual learning from action within relationships. These inner constructions guide—and limit—her feelings, thoughts, and action in all realms.

Eventually, Ann can allow only certain kinds of relationships. She can tolerate only certain feelings from others and from herself. Others must see her as only good and loving, not angry, fearful, or sad; and she must see herself this way, too. To be otherwise is to feel cast out and condemned.

Perhaps it is obvious that I've sketched some (though not all) parts of a path toward anxious, depressive immobilization and disconnection. I think that this immobilizing path underlies many women's problems, including depression itself, phobias, eating disorders, and other problems; it also leads to the so-called personality disorders such as borderline personality disorder.

In each of these situations, the woman elaborates specific images of herself and others and specific forms of action that come to seem the only possible forms of action within the framework of the relational images she has constructed. Each of these problems has its particular configurations. However, they all have grown out of attempts to find a possibility of acting within connections when the only connections available present *impossibilities*—when the people in the available relational context have threatened or actually carried out disconnections and violations of the girl's or woman's experience.

Here is a point at which Carol Gilligan and I find ourselves saying almost the same sentence (Gilligan, 1990). It makes sense that this would be so. I'm suggesting that this paradox constitutes a central core of psychological troubles. Carol Gilligan and the women working with her have contributed a powerful body of work to show us how this paradox occurs in a particularly profound way at adolescence when girls find that in order to be allowed into relationships, they have to keep large parts of themselves out of relationship. This, then, is a paradox that all women in this culture face, with profound effects on their possibilities for psychological development.

Violations

A most extreme impossibility—disconnection and violation—occurs when a woman, or even worse, a young girl, is sexually abused. The girl or woman is violated physically and psychologically, and she usually has been unable to represent the truth of her experience both within her immediate relational context and on the larger scene.

This violence represents the most severe form of the psychological violation and disconnection that can occur whenever one person (or group of people) in a relationship has greater power. A central part of this kind of domination is the power to define what can and cannot occur within relationships. These uneven relationships certainly are not based on the search for mutually empowering connections. It is obvious that in our historical tradition our formative relationships have not rested on a search for mutual empowerment. Thus, adults of both sexes have not yet been able to act within relationships in ways that fully engage with the issues in our lives and that allow us to flourish. Because adults have not had this experience, we all have difficulty in providing an optimal relational context for children.

CONCLUSION

To summarize, drawing on the work of the Stone Center and others, I've tried to review some of the major characteristics of mutually empowering relationships. I've suggested that a relational context that does not allow the developing girl or adult woman to act within relationships to represent her experience toward building mutually empathic and mutually empowering connections leads the girl or woman to construct restricted and distorted images of the possibilities of relationships between herself and others. These constructions further limit her ability to act within connections, to know her own experience, and to build a sense of worthiness.

I've suggested that girls and women who are sexually violated experience the most extreme form of a process that occurs for all women. Women who are sexually violated and the women who work with them are teaching us perhaps the most important things we need to learn at this time in order to fathom the hidden aspects of psychological development, not only of girls and women, but also of boys and men who are developing within a context that allows such widespread violence.

It's apparent that I've drawn on, but not acknowledged along the way, the thinking of many people including Freudians, object relations theorists, Kohutians, and earlier workers such as Horney and Sullivan, although I have not used such terms as "good objects," "bad objects," "part objects," or "self objects," nor self systems, false selves, or even true selves. I think that I am suggesting something very similar to Horney's concept of the "false self" and also her extraordinarily valuable elaborations of the false self, such as the idealized image and the pride system. (I do not think that the hidden, disconnected parts of a person's experience that have not grown in the course of interchange with others can compose a "true self," as some writers seem to suggest.)

Using language common to all of us—another point on which Horney offers us marvelous inspiration—I've tried to explore what happens when all the good, bad, part, and self objects come to life because—although obvious, it's rarely stated—it is women who are made into these "objects" in all the theories. Women enter the theories to supply the material by which the "subjects" build systems of "selves" and the like. When women enter the picture as persons, we move inevitably to different assumptions. I don't think we can then proceed on the premise of a self that is using the "objects" in order to develop more of a self. Instead, I think we find different premises and questions. A central question is the one with which I began: How do we create connections from the first moment of life, in which all the people involved are learning to build mutually empowering relationships? In working on such questions, we can draw on the still insufficiently recognized strengths of women.

To put this all another way, the more important work on both the personal and the global scene today is not the concentration on how the individual develops a sense of an individuated, separate self, but on how people can build empowering relationships, which, in turn, empower all of the people in those relationships.

In this sense, I believe women have an urgent and historic mission: to examine and describe still more accurately the very realm of growth-fostering relationships, which women have been trying to provide all along; to raise these to their full value, and thus, to work to redefine public visions and goals; to provide the leadership to move all of our societal structures away from systems based on violence and toward systems based on mutual empowerment.

REFERENCES

Belenky, M. F., Clinchy, B. M., Goldberger, N. R. & Tarule, J. M. (1986). *Women's Way of Knowing: The Development of Self, Voice and Mind.* New York: Basic Books.

Fairbairn, W. R. D. (1952). *An Object Relations Theory of Personality.* New York: Basic Books.

Gianino, A., & Tronick, E. (1985). In T. Field, P. McCabe, & N. Schneiderman (Eds.), *Stress and Coping.* Hillsdale, NJ: Lawrence Erlbaum.

Gilligan, C. (1982). *In a Different Voice.* Cambridge, MA: Harvard University Press.

Gilligan, C. (1987). The origins of morality in early childhood relationships. In J. Kagan & S. Lamb (Eds.), *The Emergence of Morality in Young Children.* Chicago: University of Chicago Press.

Gilligan, C. (1990). Joining the resistance: Psychology, politics, girls and women. *Michigan Quarterly Review,* 29, 501–536.

Jordan, J. (1986). The meaning of mutuality. *Work in Progress, No. 23.* Wellesley, MA: Stone Center Working Paper Series.

Jordan, J. (1987). Clarity in connection: Empathic knowing, desire and sexuality. *Work in Progress, No. 28.* Wellesley, MA: Stone Center Working Paper Series.

Kaplan, A. (1984). The self-in-relation: A theory of women's depression. *Work in Progress, No. 14.* Wellesley, MA: Stone Center Working Paper Series.

Miller, J. B. (1976). *Toward a New Psychology of Women.* Boston: Beacon Press.

Miller, J. B. (1982). Women and power. *Work in Progress, No. 1.* Wellesley, MA: Stone Center Working Paper Series.

Miller, J. B. (1986). What do we mean by relationships? *Work in Progress, No. 22.* Wellesley, MA: Stone Center Working Paper Series.

Stern, D. (1985). *The Interpersonal World of the Infant.* New York: Basic Books.

Surrey, J. (1984). The "self-in-relation": A theory of women's development. *Work in Progress, No. 13.* Wellesley, MA: Stone Center Working Paper Series.

Surrey, J. (1987). Relationship and empowerment. *Work in Progress, No. 30.* Wellesley, MA: Stone Center Working Paper Series.

7

Joining the Resistance

Psychology, Politics, Girls and Women*

CAROL GILLIGAN, Ph.D.

INTRODUCTORY NOTE

In honoring Karen Horney, I wish especially to address the spirit of her resistance and her work on women's psychology. She was the first to hear the voice of psychoanalysis as a man's voice, carrying men's fantasies and fears, and also as a voice resonant with a culture that is rooted psychologically in men's experiences. It was the dissonance between her own experience as a woman and what psychoanalysts said about women that alerted her to this truth, and her willingness to listen to herself and to take her own experience seriously is what I find most courageous in her work. This listening led

*An earlier version of this essay was presented as the Tanner Lecture on Human Values at the University of Michigan on March 16, 1990, and was later published in the *Michigan Quarterly Review* (1990), 29(4), pp. 501–536. Reprinted with permission.

her beyond the confines of existing institutions and theories and toward what Virginia Woolf saw as the contribution of women: our ability, because of the differences in our personal histories and in our relationship to society and culture, to find new words and create new methods and thus potentially to break what have been, within psychoanalysis as within the culture at large, destructive and vicious cycles.

My own work is centered in listening to women and staying with women when women's voices differ from accepted truths. In doing so, I have learned from women and come to a new understanding of psychological development and also of what it means to be human. In this approach to women and to psychology, I feel deeply joined with Jean Baker Miller. The affinity or resonances in our work have been profoundly validating personally and scientifically; working separately and in different settings, we heard similar themes in women's voices and traced a similar pathway in following women's psychological growth. This connection was brought home to us when we realized that in our papers we have written essentially the same sentence about women's psychology—Jean on the basis of her clinical work with women and the work of her colleagues at the Stone Center at Wellesley College, I on the basis of my research with women and girls and the work of my colleagues on the Harvard Project. In my version, the sentence reads: "Paradoxically, girls are taking themselves out of relationship for the sake of relationships and self-consciously letting go of themselves." This move into selflessness or voicelessness in relationships has both psychological and political consequences, just as continuing to speak when one's voice is not heard or understood or resonant with the voices of others has psychological and political costs. This relational impasse creates a crisis in women's development.

In joining women with girls, I have been working collaboratively with other women. These connections have been crucial to staying with girls and naming their dissociation from themselves—their move into not speaking and not knowing what they know. My paper grows out of this collaboration—the Harvard Project on Women's Psychology and Girls' Development. The two psychologists who appear in the paper as my traveling companions, Annie Rogers and Lyn Mikel Brown, together with Normi Noel—a theater director, actor, and voice teacher—have accompanied me most closely in this work. Elizabeth Debold, Judith Dorney, Barbara Miller, Mark Tappan, Deborah Tolman, Jill Taylor, and Janie Ward—also members of the Harvard Project—have contributed substantially to this research.

The girls who appear in this paper are students at the Atrium School, a small, innovative, coeducational private school in Watertown, Massachusetts; at the Laurel School, a girls' school in Shaker Heights, Ohio; and at a public school in the vicinity of Boston. It is important to note that although all of the girls are educationally privileged, they are not all white or all middle class. Malka and Rosie are Latina, Anna is working class, Anjli is Muslim and her family is from Lebanon. In this group of girls, color is not associated with low social class, and low social class is not associated with educational disadvantage.

I. IN THE MUSEUM

It is Tuesday. It is raining. And the Theater, Writing and Outing Club is going to the museum. Eight 11-year-old girls, members of the sixth grade at the Atrium School in Watertown, Massachusetts, and two women—Annie Rogers and myself—climb into the school van and begin to make our way through the rain-washed streets into the city. It is June. School is over for the year. The sixth grade has graduated, and the girls from the class have returned for a week of outings, writing, and theater work, designed to strengthen healthy resistance and courage. They gather in the coatroom of the Fine Arts Museum, shedding backpacks and raincoats, retrieving notebooks; they are ready. Today, I explain, they are to be investigative reporters; their assignment is to find out how girls and women appear in this museum.

"Naked," Emma says, without hesitation. A current of recognition passes swiftly, silently, through the group. Dora, one of Freud's early patients, in associating to a dream, remembers standing in the Dresden art gallery for two and a half hours in front of the Sistine Madonna. And Emma too will be transfixed by the images of women, by their nakedness in this cool, marble building. Later, when asked to write a conversation with one of the women, Emma chooses a headless, armless Greek statue, weaving into the conventions of polite childhood conversation her two burning questions: Are you cold? Would you like some clothes?[1]

But why am I telling you this story? I am interested in resistance—in healthy resistance to psychological illness, and in the relationship between political resistance and psychological resistance, both highly charged subjects in the 20th century. And I am interested more specifically in a moment of resistance that I have observed among girls at the edge of adolescence. Emma's playfully innocent, slightly irreverent conversation with the statue in the museum bespeaks her interest in the scenes that lie behind the paintings and sculpture that she is seeing—her inquiry into relationships between artists and models: what each is doing and feeling and thinking; her curiosity about the psychological dimensions of this connection between men and women. The statue's response—"I have no money"—to Emma's question as to whether she wants some clothes, reveals how readily this inquiry becomes political and sets up the dynamic I wish to follow: a tendency in girls' lives at adolescence for a healthy resistance to become a political resistance or struggle—an insistence on knowing what one knows and a willingness to be outspoken—and then for this political resistance to turn into a psychological resistance—a reluctance to know what one knows and a fear that one's experience, if spoken, will endanger relationships and threaten survival.

Freud located this intersection between psychology and politics—between the human desire for relationships and for knowledge and cultural prohibitions on loving and knowing—as a turning point in boys' early childhood and named it "the Oedipus complex," after Sophocles's tragedy about relational blindness.[2] In studying women's development, my colleagues and I have observed a comparable turning point in girls' lives at the time of adolescence.[3] This is the time when girls' desire for relationships and for knowledge comes up against the wall of Western culture and a resistance breaks out that is, I will claim, key to women's psychological health and potentially of great human value.

Let me return for a moment to the museum and record the doubling of voice and vision that characterizes girls' perception and conversation. Mame's eye for the disparity between outside and inside, between calm surface and explosive laughter, is evident as she describes the painting of *Reverend John Atwood and His Family.* His two oldest daughters, she writes, sustaining the possessive, "have no expression. They're just staring straight ahead, but one of them looks like she is going to burst out laughing." His wife, she concludes on a more somber note, "looks very worn and tired." By paying close attention to the human world around them and following the changing weather of relationships and the undercurrents of thoughts and feelings, girls come to discern patterns, to notice repeating sequences, and to hear familiar rhythms and thus find under the surface of the apparent disorder of everyday living an order that is the psychological equivalent of the Mandelbrot equations of the new chaos physics—the physics that seeks patterns of regularity within a constantly changing and relational world.

Yet girls' "unpaid-for-education"—Virginia Woolf's name for "that understanding of human beings and their motives which . . . might be called psychology"[4]—leaves girls with knowledge that often runs counter to what they are told by those in authority. So that they are left, in effect, with at least two truths, two versions of a story, two voices revealing two points of view. Malka writes not one but two conversations between herself and the Queen of Babylon. The first is the official version. Speaking in the voice of a reporter, Malka addresses the Queen in a manner befitting her station. "Hello Madam," she says to the woman in the painting who is brushing her hair while receiving news of the revolt, "What is it like ruling so great a land?" "Glorious," the Queen replies. "It is great fun, although," she adds with a yawn, "it does tax time and strength sometimes." In the second conversation, Malka speaks in her own voice to this bored, haughty Queen, asking her simply: "Whatchya doing?" The Queen, in a sudden reversal of priorities, replies: "Brushing my hair. I was interrupted this morning by a revolt."

Whose agenda, what is important, what can be spoken, and what is tacitly to be ignored—looked at but not seen, heard but not listened to? The play of girls' conversation, the questions and comments that dart in and out like minnows, followed by looks, scanning faces, and listening to what happens, seeing what follows, taking the pulse, the temperature of the human climate —Is anyone upset? What is permitted, admitted (in both senses of the word)? Conflict erupts among girls like lightning—something has happened, someone has stepped over a line. Rejection—the thin dark line of rejection: not you; we—whoever "we" are—do not want to be with you.

Girls' questions about who wants to be with whom are to them among the most important questions, and they take sharp notice throughout the day of the answers given to these questions, as revealed through nuance and gesture, voices and glances, seating arrangements, choices of partners, the responses of adult women and men, the attitudes of authorities in the world. Emma's voice in saying that the nudes are naked, Mame's voice in speaking about the irreverence of the daughter and the tiredness of the mother in Reverend John Atwood's family, Malka's voice in revealing by reversing the relationship between hair-brushing and quelling revolts are the same three voices that are suppressed in the first published version of Anne Frank's diary—the excised passages that reveal that Anne has looked at and seen her own naked body, that she has recorded disturbing thoughts and feelings about her mother, and that she knows from her reading whose activities people record and imbue with value and is disturbed by the disparate attention given to the courage and suffering of women and men. On June 15, 1944, in one of the deleted passages, she writes:

> A question that has been raised more than once and that gives me no inner peace is why did so many nations in the past, and often still now, treat women as inferior to men? Everyone can agree how unjust this is, but that is not enough for me, I would also like to know the cause of the great injustice. . . . It is stupid enough of women to have borne it all in silence for such a long time, since the more centuries this arrangement lasts, the more deeply rooted it becomes. . . . Many people, particularly women, but also men, now realize for how long this state of affairs has been wrong, and modern women demand the right of complete independence! But that's not all, respect for woman, that's going to have to come as well! . . . Soldiers and war heroes are honored and celebrated, explorers acquire

> immortal fame, martyrs are revered, but how many will look upon woman as they would upon a soldier? . . . Women are much braver, much more courageous soldiers, struggling and enduring pain for the continuance of humankind, than all the freedom-fighting heroes with their big mouths![5]

That girls' knowledge—of the body, of relationships, and of the world and its values—and girls' irreverence provide the grounds for resistance has been known since the time of *Lysistrata.* And yet Anne Frank, in what turned out to be one of the final entries in her diary—an entry that was not deleted—calls the voice of the above passage "unpleasant"; her sexuality, she says, is "insufferable," and she describes herself as living with an inner division, as being "two Annes," as having "a split personality."

II. IF ONLY WOMEN . . .

In 411 B.C.E., in the midst of the disastrous war between Athens and Sparta, Aristophanes plays out a plan for ending the war in the bawdy comedy, *Lysistrata.* If only women, he thinks, who are able to see the absurdity of men's fighting, who are wise, moreover, in the ways of human bodies and psyches, and who can have an effect on men, would take the salvation of Greece into their hands, they could, he imagines, stop the violence. At the opening of the play, Lysistrata calls the women of Athens and Sparta together, preparing to explain her plan, and the voice and expressions of this classical rendition of a peace-making woman resonate strongly with the voices and gestures of 11-year-old girls in the 20th century.

"I am angry . . . I am very angry and upset," Sarah says, protesting with her whole face and body. Somberness gathers across her eyebrows, joining them together as she says directly: "I was treated by Ted like trash." Tension is in the air. Sarah and Emma walk back and forth across the room, heads down, arms around each other's shoulders. The social texture has suddenly become dark, opaque, like sudden shadows, hurt feelings easily moving to tears and then out as talking, contact, create an opening, light and shadow, and with the play of relationships, the somberness that gathered across

Sarah's face moves off, dissipates, and the girls line up chairs, dragging them into a row, two chairs apiece, bottoms on one, feet on another, open their journals and begin writing.

"What's bothering you [Lysistrata]?" Calonice says at the beginning of Act One, in Alan Somerstein's 1973 Penguin Classics translation. "Don't screw up your face like that. It really doesn't suit you, you know, knitting your eyebrows up like a bow." "Sorry, Calonice, but I'm furious. I'm disappointed in womankind." Lysistrata is upset because the women of Athens and Sparta have not shown up for her meeting—and she knows they would do so at once for Bacchus. Calonice, taking on the task of speaking to someone who is too angry to listen, reminds Lysistrata that "it is not so easy for a wife to get out of the house."[6]

The women come, and Lysistrata explains that if women will vow to give up sex until men vow to give up fighting, they should succeed in bringing about peace—in essence by substituting the mutual pleasures of sex for men's single-minded pursuit of violence.

The strategy is as follows: the women will do everything in their power to arouse the desire of their husbands and lovers, and then they will run out of their houses and lock themselves up in the Acropolis. The plan succeeds brilliantly in the theater. The Peloponnesian War, however, continues.

More than two millennia later in Puritan New England, where the only war described is the unremitting war in the heart of the Puritans, Hawthorne puts forward a similar vision: that a woman must bring the new truth that will establish relations between women and men "on a surer ground of mutual happiness." And then, in a stunning exegesis, with the brilliant economy of a single letter, demonstrates why this vision is bound to eventuate in failure. The very knowledge and passion that enable a woman to escape from "the iron framework of [men's] reasoning" also disable her, by causing her to be labeled an impure woman: a woman who has been adulterated.[7]

This double vision that at once enables and imprisons women is explicated in the chapter entitled, "Another View of Hester," after seven-year-old Pearl, in "The Minister's Vigil," trenchantly gives another view of the Reverend Arthur Dimmesdale ("Thou wast not bold! . . . thou wast not true! . . . Thou wouldst not promise to take my hand, and mother's hand tomorrow noontide!").[8] The scarlet letter, the narrator explains, revealing Hester's passion and also her knowledge of relationships that the Puritan eye cannot discern, gives her "so much power to do and power to sympathize . . . with her fellow creatures," that many people said that the A meant Able rather than Adultery, "so strong was Hester Prynne with a woman's strength."[9]

Living at once inside and outside the framework, Hester is able to see the frame. The "lawless passion" that broke the bonds of convention and released her from the chain of the good, enabled her mind to run free—leading to silent speculation that, the narrator surmises, the Puritan forefathers "would have held to be a deadlier crime than that stigmatized by the scarlet letter," a crime that threatened not simply her own position but the very foundation of the Puritan order.[10]

Like the hysterical women of the late 19th century—the women whose features Freud lists in describing his early patient, Fräulein Elisabeth von R., noting as characteristic "her giftedness, her ambition, her moral sensibility, her excessive demand for love which, to begin with, found satisfaction in her family, and the independence of her nature which went beyond the feminine ideal and found expression in a considerable amount of obstinacy, pugnacity and reserve"[11]—Hester Prynne has the character of a resister: "a mind of native courage and ability," a woman whom fate and fortune had set free.

> The scarlet letter was her passport into regions where other women dared not tread. Shame, Despair, Solitude! These had been her teachers—stern and wild ones—and they had made her strong, but taught her much amiss.[12]

In the end, then, she must be corrected—and unlike Dora, Freud's later patient who flees from what had become the iron framework of his treatment, leaving her analysis in midstream, Hester, in the dark conclusion to Hawthorne's brooding novel, takes on the Puritan mantle. Assuring the women who come to her for counsel and comfort that a new truth will reveal a new order of living and that "the angel and apostle of the coming revelation must be a woman," she explains that this woman—whom she once thought might be herself—must in contrast be "lofty [and] pure" as well as beautiful, and "wise not through dusky grief, but the ethereal medium of joy . . . and sacred love."[13] Thus the very woman who is able to envision a new order of human relations is, by the same token, unable since the experience that enables her also adulterates her in the eyes of the community. Released from goodness, she is imprisoned in badness, within the iron framework of a puritanical order.

This imprisonment of women becomes the subject of Claudia Koonz's scathing jeremiad—her 1987 study of women in Nazi Germany, which she entitles, *Mothers in the Fatherland.* Koonz asks on a political level the question that currently rivets psychotherapists: how could women, how could mothers especially, have stayed with and supported such fathers? Interviewing Gertrude Scholtz-Klink, the "Lady Führer über Alles" who was chief of the Women's Bureau—the oxymoronic Nazi social service agency—and author of *Woman in the Third Reich*, Koonz is spellbound by her protestations of goodness, by a moral piety and smugness that seemingly admit no pity. "Crimefeel" is the term she coins for this unrepentant woman's insistence on describing herself as both a good mother and a good Nazi—the emotional analogue to the murderous "crimethink" that Orwell describes in *1984*. That women did not resist Hitler in any more significant numbers than did doctors, clergy, professors, and others is surprising only in that the main form that resistance could take under the relentless eye of the Nazi terror was, it would seem, characteristically female, falling into "what we think of as 'women's work'"—grounded less in the rhetoric of heroism than in a realistic sense of vulnerability, involving "manipulat[ion] [of] the situation, intelligence and the ability to assess the enemy's personality."[14] Yet women as a group did not do this work but instead actively supported and voted into power the openly sexist and avowedly misogynistic Nazi Party, with an idealization of mothers that provided only the thinnest of veils over the underlying rage and contempt. Soldiers and mothers—the imagery of Hitler's Germany: What were they doing in one another's company?

The relationship between soldiers and mothers surfaces in the very different context of Diana Russell's 1989 study, *Lives of Cour-*

age: Women for a New South Africa, creating a paradox that Russell highlights for her reader. Interviewing politically courageous women, Russell heard repeatedly about the importance of women in the resistance movement and the extraordinary strength and resilience of women not only in the face of daily adversity, but also under the extreme conditions of political detention and torture. Many women in one way or another echoed Albertina Sisulu's conviction that "women are the people who are going to relieve us from this oppression and depression."[15] Yet when asked why there are relatively few women leaders, these same women referred to "women's internalized sense of inferiority, their poor education, their lack of assertiveness, and the strong beliefs in traditional gender roles that still prevail in African cultures." She finds it difficult, Russell tells her reader,

> to reconcile these two perspectives. The fact that only 5 percent to 12 percent of the political detainees are women suggests that women are underrepresented not only in leadership positions but also in the rank-and-file of the movement.[16]

Her discussion then turns to the crucial role women play in enabling men to be politically active and also to the fact that women are mothers and often faced with raising children single-handedly and providing for them on severely inadequate wages. Like Anne Frank, Russell laments the inattention given to mothers' courage and bravery. And yet, this leaves unanswered the question that Virginia Woolf raises in *Three Guineas*: Is there a way in which women can help men prevent rather than wage what has historically been the male act of war—the violence which, whatever its causes, leaves in its wake a litter of dead bodies and ruined houses?

In her darkly cautious and brilliantly far-reaching address to this question, Woolf gently shifts the focus of attention away from mothers and to the "daughters of educated men," for whom she lays out a three-step passage out of the private house of their fathers and into the public world where they will form a "Society of Outsiders." The steps that Woolf sees as essential are university education and admission to the professions so that women can gain what is to be their only weapon: the power of independent opinion supported by independent income. Because women's experiences in living and women's relation to the tradition differ from men's, women may succeed in "finding new words and creating new methods,"[17] and thus may help men to break what otherwise is a vicious cycle.

The dangers inherent in this process Woolf calls "adultery of the brain" and "brain-selling" or writing "what you do not want to write for the sake of money" (or other forms of status and power). Through these practices, women create and let loose upon the world "anaemic, vicious and diseased progeny," which then infect others, spreading ways of seeing and speaking that women know to be untrue or unreal.[18]

The deeply knotted dilemma, then, that lies at the center of women's development is how can girls both enter and stay outside of, be educated in, and then change what has been for centuries a man's world? And yet, since "the public and the private worlds are inseparably connected . . . [and since] the tyrannies and servilities of the one are the tyrannies and servilities of the other," since we live in one world and cannot dissociate ourselves from one another, and since the psychology of fathers that has ruled the private house is writ large in legal codes and moral orders and supported by the ever-present threat of what is considered to be a legitimate use of force or violence, how can daughters be anywhere other than inside and outside of these structures?[19]

Girls' doubling of voice and vision is a response to a psychologically untenable split between what girls know through experience and what is socially constructed as reality. As girls move from childhood into adolescence and from primary into secondary education, they are under intense internal and external pressure to modulate their voices and to correct their vision and thus to align themselves with cultural traditions, so that they can enter without changing what has been called "the human conversation." With this seemingly simple change of voice, girls' voices are said to sound pleasing; girls' ability to shift their point of view—to correct their perspective, like making a correction in a geometry problem or algebraic equation—is generally taken simply as a mark of cognitive maturity or psychological development rather than a move that leaves girls in danger of losing voice and perspective. For once this correction for voice and vision is made, the cultural framework becomes invisible, and then, in the words of one wise 12-year-old girl, "you don't have to think."

In an extraordinary film about South Africa, which has the slow-motion quality of recovering memory, Shawn Slovo begins to think out loud, as it were, about what it means to be a mother. In doing so, she returns to the year when she was 13, the year when her mother was taken away to prison, and considers in the context of this most difficult moment in their relationship with one another, "how to merge the politics with the personal without detracting from the importance of either."[20] Slovo is the daughter of Ruth First, the journalist who was one of the few whites centrally involved with the African National Congress, a woman whose militant opposition to Apartheid led her to be arrested and detained for 90 days twice by the South African government in 1963, the year of the film's action. In 1982, Ruth First was killed by a parcel bomb while working with the resistance in Mozambique.

Set at that edge of girls' development, that moment when childhood falls into adolescence, *A World Apart* catches an angle of perception that is at odds with conventional ways of speaking about mothers and daughters. In portraying a mother in relation to her adolescent daughter rather than a little girl, the film deeply calls into question conventional images of and ideas about good and bad mothers and mothering. And this shift in perspective is, inadvertently, a discovery Slovo makes in the course of making the film. Slovo, in her introduction to the diary she kept in the course of her writing, records that she set out to speak in essentially conventional terms about the conflict between a mother's political involvement and her daughter's needs. The film, she says, is about

> the relationship between a white woman, politically committed to the fight against Apartheid, and her thirteen-year-old daughter who must contend against politics for the love, care and time of her mother. Set against the backdrop of increasingly violent repression, [the film] chronicles the effects of the break-up of the family.[21]

And yet Slovo writes a very different screenplay. Showing the break-up of "the family," she chronicles the connection between mother and daughter, which follows from the daughter's insistence on entering the emotional center of her mother's life. Thirteen-year-old Molly, in the film's central scene, literally breaks her mother's silence, by opening her secret drawer and reading her diary. What she discovers is what she most feared—that her mother had "tried to leave us," that she had tried to kill herself in prison. Confronting her mother with this relational betrayal, she says: "You don't care about us. You shouldn't have had us."[22]

In writing out this accusation of bad mothering—an accusation forcefully made by Pauline Kael and other critics—Slovo hears her mother's voice as well as her own. And the scene that she had resisted writing was "the conversation, the confrontation, my mother and I had never had"—what remained unspoken between them and which "in life . . . was what kept us apart." What Slovo discovers, in writing out this scene, is that what she knew and did not know that she knew about her relationship with her mother turns out to have been "there all the time, just waiting for the last moment."[23]

The scene for Slovo has the quality of remembering. For me, working with girls and women of this age, it has the ring of familiarity resonating with other moments when daughters fight for relationships with their mothers and mothers let them in. Then the desire for authentic or real connection overrides the restraints on relationships between mothers and daughters that have been upheld by cultural icons of good and bad women (Madonnas and whores). In the case of Shawn Slovo, this leads her to a reformulation of her basic question about the relationship between the personal and the political: What does it mean to be a good mother to an adolescent daughter, coming of age in a violent and racist society? and What can women teach girls about resistance and courage and love in the face of indifference, cruelty, and violence?

The illusion that blinds the critics is seen through in the course of the film; mothers and daughters do not and cannot live in a world apart. Slovo steadily directs the viewer's eye to the enclosure—the imprisonment of conventionally good South African white women behind the elaborate fences of their private schools and houses.

Mothers, she shows, cannot stay with their daughters without joining the resistance, at least once their daughters are able to see beyond this enclosure, *and* yet daughters and mothers need to find ways to stay with one another in this struggle.

III. RESISTANCE

Five psychological truths:[24]

1. What is unvoiced or unspoken, because it is out of relationship, tends to get out of perspective and to dominate psychic life.
2. The hallmarks of loss are idealization and rage, and under the rage, immense sadness. ("To want and want and not to have." Virginia Woolf, *To the Lighthouse.*)
3. What is dissociated or repressed—known and then not known—tends to return, and return, and return.
4. The logic of the psyche is an associative logic—the free-falling logic of dreams, poetry, and memory—as well as a formal logic of classification and control.
5. One learns the answers to one's own questions; what one asks shapes what one knows.

Anna at 12, tall, thin, her dark hair cut short, her green eyes looking steadily out of a quiet and somewhat wary face, raises the question: How can you tell if what people are saying is true, "if what they are saying about you, if they really mean it, or if they are just doing it to be mean, and it's hard to tell, I mean, with a lot of people you can't tell how they are." What she is trying to understand is the truth of relationships—more specifically, the difference between the surface banter of teasing, making fun, putting people down, which went on among her friends (although she does not know if they were really her friends) at the public school she went to, and being mean, "really mean," or cruel. At her new school—a girls' school, Anna notices that everyone is "nice," and she feels good about herself when she is "nice to people or . . . not being mean," and bad about herself when she is mean or hurts people but "sometimes you just can't help it." Anna feels that people can tell how she feels, even when "inside I'm really sad about something but outside I'm trying to be happy," because "if you're feeling sad, you just can't make yourself happy."[25]

Malka writes about the disparity between inside and outside after the outing club's trip to Plum Island—a beach and bird sanctuary on Boston's north shore:

> A sand castle, life on a small scale. Kingdoms rise and fall, water ebbs in and out. Water rises, in and out. Channels, pools, castles, forests. The outside view. But on the inside—are babies being born? Are children playing? Are crafts being learned? Are people being married? Are battles being fought? Are people dying? Love, fun, smiling, and crying. Life. A sand castle.

At the edge of adolescence, girls draw attention to the disparity between an insider's view of life, which they are privy to in childhood, and an outside view, intimating that the insider's knowledge is in danger of being washed out or giving way. The connection between inside and outside becomes explicitly a focus of attention when girls reach adolescence and become subjected to a kind of voice and ear training, designed to make it clear what voices people like to listen to in girls and what girls can say without being called, in today's vernacular, "stupid," or "rude." On a daily basis, girls receive lessons on what they can let out and what they must keep in, if they do not want to be spoken about by others as mad or bad or simply told they are wrong. Anna, dealing with this problem of containment, says that she would like to be "just a better person or have better ways of thinking" and explains:

> Sometimes I will get really mad, and I can outburst or something, and I can't be like that . . . I have to learn how to work with people, *because sometimes I just get really mad at people who can't understand what I am saying*, and I get so exasperated. It is like, "Why can't you just . . .? What's wrong with you? Why can't you see this my way?" And I have to really go

> for what I want, though. I can't let this stuff take over me. And I have to, you kind of have to fight to get what you want. [emphasis added]

In essence, Anna states the problem of resistance as a problem of relationship. She feels pressure to hold herself in, "not to be like that . . . [not to] get really mad," or, even worse, "outburst." At the same time, she realizes she must not let go of what she wants, that "I can't let this stuff take over me." One resistance is psychological and will lead Anna to take herself out of relationship, not to fight for the understanding she wants but to become "nice" and as she now views it, "successful." The other resistance is political, and by staying in relationship, Anna will come into conflict with others.

Anna struggles between these two forms of resistance at the age of 12. With her mother, she experiences the central dilemma of relationship: how to speak honestly—to stay in connection with what she feels and knows—and also to stay in connection with others' feelings and knowledge. When they go shopping for clothes, Anna explains,

> She will pull something out and she'll say, "Well, what do you think of it?" And then if I say I don't like it, then she'll get really mad, and she'll put it back. . . . And then, she'll forget about what happens when I really give her my opinion, and then she'll say, "Tell me what you really think about it." And then she gets mad when I tell her. . . . And I'll say, "Well, you don't really want it because you already screamed at me when I gave it."

Eleven-year-old Tessie articulates the importance of voicing conflicts in relationships, explaining why it is necessary to "tell someone about it" so that you are "telling it from both sides" and can "*hear* the [other] person's point of view."

> When you are having an argument . . . and you just keep it inside you and don't tell anyone, you never hear the other person's point of view. And if you are telling someone about

> it, you are telling it from both sides and so you hear what my mother said, or what my brother said. And the other person can say, well, you might be mad, but your mom was right, and you say, yeah, I know. So when you say it out loud, you have to listen.

Tessie also observes that fighting—by which she means verbal conflict or voicing disagreement—is good for relationships: "fighting is what makes relationships go on," in the face of trouble, and "the more fights you get in and the more it goes on . . . the stronger it gets because the more you can talk with that person." The subtlety of Tessie's understanding of how people come to know one another and what kind of knowledge is necessary if friends are not to hurt one another's feelings is evident as she explains that it is through fighting, rather than "just saying 'I'm sorry' to them," that you learn "how that person feels," and then you know how "not to hurt their feelings." Yet fights also carry with them the danger of not speaking and "then you seem to grow apart."[26]

I emphasize this detailed, specific psychological knowledge—this relational knowing—based on careful listening and sustained relationship and characterized by finely wrought distinctions—a naturalist's rendering of the human world—because girls' love and girls' knowledge when brought into the public world are readily dismissed as trivial or seen as transgressive, with the result that girls are told repeatedly not to speak, not to say anything, or at least not to talk in public about what they want to know.

When Anna is interviewed at age 13, as an eighth grader, her interview is peppered with the phrase "I don't know" (spoken now over three times as often as the previous year, increasing from 21 times at age 12 to 67 times at age 13, with no corresponding increase in the length of the interview transcript). Anna is struggling explicitly with a reluctance to know what she wants to know and an inclination to suppress her feelings and thoughts and to go along with the group. Asked about whether she has work that she loves, this child who loves learning and loves school says "reading and singing . . . and I can just sort of get lost in them and not have to think about things." Talking about herself as a knower, she observes that "you can interpret things differently" and describes the way thoughts and feelings cascade differently from different beginnings, so that depending on where you start from—for example in reading a poem—you arrive at different endpoints.

But now conformity has a hold on Anna as she begins to feel like a member of her new school, not only a top student but also a part of her class. She watches others to see which way to go and does not, she says, "massively disagree on anything." With friends, if she disagreed, she would be "kind of mad at myself, have kind of a messed up feeling." With adults, "they would overpower me most of the time." Anna is learning to bring herself into line with the world around her, to bring herself into agreement with others so as not to mess up relationships with friends or experience the helplessness of being overpowered by adults. Paradoxically, for the sake of relationship and also for protection, she is disconnecting her self from others.

At 14, in ninth grade, Anna bursts out. Becoming outspoken, she draws the interviewer's attention to the change she hears in her voice: "I used to be really quiet and shy and everything, and now I am really loud." Again, the phrase "I don't know" has increased dramatically (from 67 to 135 times),[27] but now it alternates with the phrase "you know," punctuating a tale of resistance that is clearly political: Anna's insistence on knowing what she knows and writing the paper she wants to write, even though she knows it will make her English teacher angry. "I see things from a lot of points of view," Anna explains, and calling her ability to see from different viewpoints "creative" now rather than "crazy," she tells the following story.

The class was asked to write a hero legend, and Anna did not see the hero in the same way as her teacher. In Anna's rendition of the teacher's viewpoint: "There was a ladeedah hero who went and saved all humankind." Anna, however, sees this hero from a different standpoint:

> I wanted to write it from a Nazi standpoint, like Hitler as hero, and she really did not go for that at all. And I started to write, and she got really mad, and she was, like, I am afraid you are going to come out sounding like a little Nazi . . .

Anna's solution was to write two papers, two versions of the hero legend: "a ladeedah legend and the one I wanted to write." She turned both papers into her teacher along with a letter explaining her reasons. "She gave me an A on the normal one. I gave her the other one because I just had to write it. It sort of made me mad."

Anna wrote about Hitler "from the point of view of a little boy who was joining one of those groups that they had, and he was so proud to have a uniform and he went to try to salute. . . . It did not come out about Hitler as much as about the reasons for Hitler,"—which interested Anna, who was part German and whose father had been unemployed. In addition, Anna has seen, by watching her father and her brothers easily resort to what she calls "brute force" in the face of frustration, how the need to appear strong or heroic can cover over vulnerability and lead to violence. To Anna, the hero legend is an understandable but dangerous legend.

In choosing to disagree openly with her teacher and, in Woolf's terms, not to sell her writing or commit adultery of the brain, Anna said she was "just really mad" and that her teacher "was just narrow-minded" in her insistence that Hitler was an "antihero" rather than a hero.

"It was an urge," Anna says, "I had to write that paper because I was so mad. . . . I had to write it to explain it to her, you know; I just had to. . . . I just had to make her understand."

This urgent need to "make her understand," the overwhelming desire for human connection—to bring one's own inner world of thoughts and feelings into relationship with the thoughts and feelings of others—feels very pressing to girls who fight for authentic relationships and who resist being shut up, put down, turned away, ignored. Anna's friend went to talk with the teacher on Anna's behalf, and her mother encouraged her to write the paper but to do so in a way that would not antagonize the teacher. In the end, Anna concludes that her teacher "probably saw it as more annoying than anything else." What she learned from this experience, she said, "was not to antagonize people," her mother's caution. In fact, she was able both to speak and to not antagonize people—in part, she suspects, because she had not been heard, because her teacher did not understand, but also because her teacher, however annoyed, was willing to listen and read both papers.

Anna at 14 sees the framework of the worlds she lives in. Painfully, she has become aware of the inconsistencies in the school's position on economic differences—where money is available and where it isn't, the limits of the meritocracy that is espoused. And seeing inconsistencies, she becomes riveted by the disparity between the names of things and the realities, and she plays with the provocation of being literal in an effort to call things by their right names.

At 15, Anna begins to ask some literal questions about the order that is taken to be unquestionable in the world she lives in—questions about religion and violence. And she discovers that her questions are not welcomed by many of her classmates, and her opinions are often met with silence; in the midst of an intensely controversial classroom conversation, she notices who is not speaking: "There were a bunch of people who just sat there like stones and listened."

Anne Frank in one of the suppressed diary entries, comments on the silences that surround the subject of sex. On March 18, 1944, at the age of 14, she writes:

> Parents and people in general are very strange when it comes to [sexual matters]. Instead of telling their daughters as well as their sons everything when they are 12 years old, they send the children out of the room during such conversations and leave them to find things out for themselves. If the parents notice later on that the children have learned things anyway, then they assume that the children know either more or less than they actually do. . . . Grownups do come up against an important obstacle, although I'm sure the obstacle is no more than a very small barrier, they believe that children will stop looking on marriage as something sacred and pure when it dawns on them that in most cases the purity is nothing more than eyewash.[28]

What puzzles Anna is the reluctance of people to speak about cruelty and violence. Like Anne Frank, she notes the readiness of adults to cover over what they do not want children to look at—so that girls, especially as they reach adolescence, are encouraged, tacitly, not to know what they see, or not to listen to what they hear, or to see everything as "nice." And yet Anna is also bothered by her mother's refusal to wash over the realities of her life and confused by what she is taking in—in part because of the disparity between what women are saying in the two worlds that she lives in.

The acuity of Anna's perception is striking. She sees in her family what Glen Elder and Avshalom Caspi saw in studying families living under economic hardship, where fathers are unemployed and emotionally volatile and mothers and daughters bond. Anna's family constellation (herself and younger brothers) matches the picture for maximal psychological risk, given the consistent finding that when families are under stress, the children who are more psychologically in danger are boys in childhood and girls at adolescence.[29] Anna's confiding relationship with her mother thus seems critical to Anna's resilience. The closeness between them and the openness of their conversation exposes Anna to painful feelings. Anna feels her mother's feelings "gnawing at me." And she finds it confusing to take in her mother's experience, to know how her mother thinks and feels, and also to listen to other people. She realizes that her mother's is "only one viewpoint," and she does not "know how much of it is dramatized." Still, she "can see that a lot of what my mom says is true."

"You can't see someone like my dad," she says, as an 11th grader in the fifth year of the study, returning to the question that she raised at the outset, "without realizing how easily people are taken in." At school, she has "gotten a glimpse" behind the scenes and seen women whom she thought were nice and compassionate "give away their color," after which, she astutely observes, "all you can see is that part." "It is awful," she continues, describing the chameleonlike way in which her father changes his voice when he answers the phone, thus covering over the reality of what is going on in the family:

> In the midst of screaming and yelling and ranting and raving at everyone in our house, the phone rings: "Hello"—like that.

> And it is really awful. Everyone thinks he is the strongest person, and when you see the other side, you just get so annoyed when people do that.

"I could," Anna muses, "probably give *the* best senior speech in the world in terms of shocking people, but people just don't, you know, it is so different, because there is just no one," she says with adolescent fervor, "no one who has to deal with anywhere near the same thing [as I do]." The violent outbursts of her father toward her brothers have brought social service agencies to the house; her brother's violence toward her mother has brought the police. Because of the social class difference, Anna may think that hers is the only family (in her school) where violence happens. And yet, she concludes, "Pollyanna"—that epitome of the nice girl—"would have problems. . . . Thinking that life is peaches and cream is not realistic. It's not real. . . . It really grates on you when you have someone around you that is like Pollyanna . . . that is really scary, you know; you can't deal with someone like that." The niceness that governs and sustains the school that she goes to cannot admit the world that Anna knows from experience . . . and Anna knows it. They are, she says, "totally different outlooks on life."

"The real world," Anna begins, ". . . I have a bunch of friends that I talk to and, you know, they understand and everything, but it is not very many people. This school," she concludes, "is not the real world." Anna, who loves school, who wants to take everything that there is to take, to know everything she can know about the world—to know Chinese and Latin as well as French and English—does not know how to imagine her future: whether she will enter the world that the people in her school think of as "normal"—the world that is reflected in the norms—or whether she will join Woolf's Outsiders' Society and armed with an independent income to support her independent opinions,

> will be one of those people who go through college and get a Ph.D. and I'll live at the bottom of a mountain in Montana. Just one of those weird people. Have a chicken farm. I don't know. Then I will just write books or something,

remaining, as Woolf envisioned, "outside (and) experiment[ing] not with public means in public but with private means in private."[30]

IV. PSYCHOLOGY AND POLITICS: PERFECT GIRLS AND DISSIDENTS

"The anxious bird," Jorie Graham writes in her poem, "The Age of Reason,"

...........in the wild
spring green
is *anting*, which means,
in my orchard
he has opened his wings
over a furious
anthill and will take up
into the delicate
ridges of quince-yellow
feathers
a number of tiny, angry
creatures

that will inhabit him, bewildered
no doubt,
travelling deep
into the air
on this feathery planet
new life . . .

We don't know why
they do it.
At times they'll take on
almost anything
that burns, spreading
their wings

over coals, over cigarette
butts,
even, mistakenly, on bits
of broken glass.
Meanwhile the light keeps
stroking them

as if it were love.

The poem is an inquiry about love. Love means opening; it means taking in vulnerability. And Graham asks the question: What, in the name of love, is taken in? The world of nature, with its ever-present reminder of death—"The garden / continues its work / all round them, the gradual / openings that stand / for death." And the world humans cultivate, the stories that grow in the hothouse of culture: "Under the plastic / groundcover the human / garden grows: help-sticks / and knots, row / after row. Who wouldn't want / to take / into the self / something that burns / or cuts, or wanders / lost / over the body?"

Who would, or wouldn't, in the name of love, take in films like Werner Herzog's *Woyzeck*, where

the hero whom
we love
who is mad has
murdered

the world, the young
woman
who is his wife,
and loved her,
and covered himself
with blood,

he grows frightened
by how quickly
she softens and takes on the shape
of the soil.

The emphasized lines, the short lines of this poem, in their staccato insistence telling, flashing, a warning to women, like Emilia in the brothel scene of *Othello* desperately trying to tell Desdemona before it is too late what she needs to know about what Othello is thinking, and feeling, Graham's words capturing the essence of that warning, like nautical flags flying or newspaper headlines: *murdered / woman / and loved her / with blood.* How often, how far do we take this truth in? How do philosophers reason about this, what are reasonable answers to the poet's questions: "How far is true / enough? / How far into the earth / can vision go and / still be / love?"[31]

When 11-year-old Tessie is asked, at the end of November, what stays with her in looking back over the past year, she says, "the summer, things that we do in the summer . . . like the sailing that we do and all the fun that I had going swimming and doing different things." Asked how she would describe herself to herself, Tessie says simply, "I like myself." Pleasure runs through Tessie's life like water flowing, swirling around her friends in the summer, her fights with her brother, swimming, reading, writing stories, her closeness with her mother, her special relationship with her father who "always wanted a daughter," her confidence and pleasure—in taking care of children, in throwing sawdust on a classmate who has made her angry, in deciding it was worth it to get into trouble, in helping people with difficult things or problems, in meeting new people, "that's fun, you get to know more people as you go on."

But Tessie also has taken in, in the name of love, an image of perfection, exemplified by her grandmother, the person she admires:

> She is *always* smiling and *always* laughing. She's *always* doing something helpful. I don't know. She goes to a nursing home, and she writes letters for people who can't write letters. . . . She *always* has things made and *always* has little things for little kids. . . . She makes big terrariums and everything that she sells at the Church fair, and she enjoys what she is doing, she loves her grandchildren and her children. And she seems to be an *always* happy person and *always* willing to help you and everything. [emphasis added]

The repeated word, "always," catches the stillness at the center of this frozen image; Tessie's free-flowing world has suddenly stopped.

Ellen, at 11, asked whether there is someone whom she admires, describes a variant of this image—a perfect girl who seems an offshoot of the always good woman, and the repeated word "really" in her description suggests that Ellen may be questioning whether what she is seeing is real.

> There is this girl in our class who is perfect . . . She's *really* tall, not *really* tall, she's tall, and is pretty and she's good at everything. You could say something, and she could do it perfectly. And she's smart, and she is good at any sport, and she's good at art, and she's good at everything. She's like a person I know, like my mother's friend in college. She's good at everything. There is not one thing she cannot do. She's *really* nice and . . . she's *always* being herself.

Claudia, the astute nine-year-old narrator of Toni Morrison's novel, *The Bluest Eye*, sums up "this disrupter of seasons," the girl who appears in the elementary school classroom late and "enchanted the entire school."[32]

The familiarity of this girl, her regular appearance at the edge of adolescence in girls' lives and in women's novels, signals a shift in the cultural framework that is key to the psychology and politics of girls' adolescence. Suddenly girls feel the presence of a standard that does not come out of their experience and an image that, because embodied, calls into question the reality that they have lived in—the moving, changing world of thoughts and feelings, relationships and people. Feeling the mesmerizing presence of the perfect girl, girls have entered the world of the hero-legend and experience the imposition of a framework that seemingly comes out of nowhere—a world view superimposed on girls but grounded in the psychology of men. With the arrival of the perfect girl, who exemplifies the incredible, girls are in danger of losing their world. But they are also in danger, in the world of the hero legend, if they continue to know what they know and especially if they say it in public. What once seemed ordinary to girls—speaking, difference, anger, conflict, fighting, bad as well as good thoughts and feelings—now seems treacherous: laced with danger, a sign of imperfection, a harbinger of being left out, not chosen.

Like the hero or the superheroes of boys' early childhood, the perfect girl of girls' early adolescence is an emblem of loss—signifying an idealization that replaces relationship, covering over a rage that is unspeakable and a sadness that seems endless, and thus marking an inner division or psychic chasm: a taking of the self out of relationship in the name of love. This is the move enacted by the hand that censored Anne Frank's diary, removing her slightly from the reader (especially the puritanical American reader), imposing a kind of innocence or psychological virginity, so that she—who knew so much—would appear more perfect or more acceptable or more protected in the eyes of the world by seeming to know less than she knew. The evidence covered over reveals the extent of Anne's connection with her body, with desire, with her mother, and with the world she lived in—a world that contained both the story of Woyzeck and the Nazis. Living in the midst of real terror, she had not lost her world.

If girls' knowledge of reality is politically dangerous, it is both psychologically and politically dangerous for girls not to know what is going on—or to render themselves innocent by disconnecting themselves from their bodies, that repository of experience and desire, and thus, in essence, disassociating themselves from themselves, from relationships and from what they know about the world. Because girls are encouraged to make this disconnection at the time of their adolescence, girls' dissent at this time becomes psychologically essential and potentially healing for boys as well. And yet at adolescence, girls' knowledge and girls' passion are bound to make trouble in the world girls are entering.

When Rosie is interviewed at age 14, her vitality is infectious. She speaks openly in the privacy of the interview setting about desire as sexual—in somewhat the same tentative yet resolute manner that Anne Frank describes in preparing to speak about her body ("When the subject [of what a naked girl looks like] comes up again," she says to herself in her diary, "how in heaven's name will you be able to explain what things are like [down there] without using examples? Shall I try it out here in the meantime? Well then get on with it!")[33] Rosie's pleasure in her body and her exuberance at age 14 are unmistakable. At the same time, she is in trouble at school for her outspokenness, her irreverence, and her refusal, despite her evident brightness, to be the perfect student.

At 15, Rosie and her boyfriend are caught in the park by a ranger who calls her mother to come and take Rosie home. Rosie was embarrassed and scared about what was going to happen to her, and also worried about disillusioning her mother who "had this image of me . . . as close to the perfect child." Asked to describe this perfect child, she says, without hesitation: "She gets straight A's and has a social life, but still gets home exactly on the dot, on time, and does everything her parents say, and keeps her room neat." I ask Rosie: "Are there girls like this?" She says, "Perhaps; saints." "Do saints have sex?" I wonder, thinking of Rosie. "I don't know," she begins, and then fills in her solution: "If they want, as long as they don't get caught; as long as nobody knows."

Once her mother knew, Rosie "hunted her down and . . . made her talk to me. And it wasn't like a battle or anything. . . . I just wanted to talk to her and see what she had to say." Like Anna who wants to connect her own with her teacher's view of the hero, by "making her understand," Rosie wants to discover what connections are possible between herself and her mother, what her mother is willing to say.

Rosie's clarity, her playfulness, her irreverence in refusing to disembody saints, and her courage in staying in her own body coexist with confusion about the world she lives in.

Despite her efforts, she cannot find the emotional center—the place where desire or passion or pleasure live in her mother's busy life. From her mother, she takes in the caution that she must be more careful about her body, more attentive to the warning signals and the flags of danger. Perhaps the seemingly disembodied perfect girl who her mother and teachers envision she could be really exists and is admirable, exemplifying the way Rosie should live in order to take care of herself in a world where imperfection often means rejection and where, more darkly, sex can be fatal, love can mean murder, and fighting can mean violence.

At the end of *Oedipus Rex*, that psychological telling of the hero legend, after the truth about family relations has been uncovered (that Oedipus has unwittingly murdered his father and married his mother, and that it was his mother who [cannily, uncannily?] gave him away to the herdsman), Oedipus blinds himself, Jocasta strangles herself, their sons run off to become kings and war against one another, and their daughters are summoned to accompany their father in his blindness. A quick scanning of Sophocles' *tableau vivant* of life in the patriarchal family suggests that the wounds that fathers suffer in early childhood infect their daughters in adolescence. Yet in a play that is filled with riddles and questions—where the chorus asks about Jocasta's silence ("How could the Queen whom Lauis won, / Be silent when that deed was done?"),[34] no one asks on behalf of the daughters: Why did Oedipus blind himself?

V. WOMEN TEACHING GIRLS/ GIRLS TEACHING WOMEN

It is September, and the sky over New England is Fra Angelico blue. With Lyn Mikel Brown I am flying to Cleveland, to talk with the Laurel School teachers about our research with the girls they are teaching.[35] It is the beginning of the second year of the project, and the library fills as we enter, the faculty sitting in short rows crossing the room, with a long aisle running down the center. School—the microcosm in children's lives of the public world, the public space that Hannah Arendt sees as the crucible of democracy, the place where the natality and plurality, the ever new and always different nature of the human condition can flourish.

The school is governed by an honor code, which is working well according to the school's recent evaluation, maintaining an order of living where people can bring themselves and leave their things in safety. In the privacy of the research interview, girls speak about the honor code from a different angle, describing dilemmas of relationship that arise in the wake of honor code violations; how, they wonder, can they stay in connection with themselves and also be in connection with others? Since there seems no way to speak about these problems of relationship in the public arena, many girls publicly agree to an honor code that they do not believe in.[36] And, taking matters of public governance into their own hands, girls take them into a private world of relationships and settle them in private places, drawing on that psychological knowledge—that intricate physics of relationship that girls learn by keeping an eye on the human weather and following the constant play of relationships as it moves across the sky of the day.

This girls' school, like a perfectly run household, is being governed as if effortlessly. In fact, it is run by an underground society of girls whose knowledge and activities on behalf of the school are for the most part unseen and unnamed. Speaking to the assembled faculty, I observe that if their goal is to educate girls who as women will participate fully as citizens in a democratic state, then it seems necessary to bring girls' questions about public governance into the public arena—to name girls' relational activities and knowledge that are responsible for maintaining the public safety and also to encourage girls to speak publicly of their differences and to voice their disagreement.

To my right, in front, a woman—small bones, white hair, intense face concentrating energy as her thoughts and feelings connect with sound and come out into the air of the room on her voice—says: "How can we help girls learn to deal with disagreement in public, when we"—she looks across the rows, quickly scanning the faces of her colleagues, women and men—"when we," meaning now women, "cannot deal with disagreement in public ourselves?"

Silence washed the room. The research was uncovering the underground. Girls' voices, recorded in private and amplified in the public space of the school, were resonating with women teachers, encouraging women to ask: what were they teaching girls about relationships, about speaking, about conflict, about difference, about political and psychological resistance?

Two questions about relationships are clarifying for women: Where am I in relation to the traditions I am practicing or teaching, what do I think is worth knowing or passing on, and where am I in relation to girls, the next generation of women? Are women vessels through which cultures pass? Are women oracles of the disciplines, conveying, like the priestess who was the oracle of Apollo, the wisdom of male gods? Provocative questions, but it was the relationship between girls and women that proved to be transformative, and most specifically, the relationship of women to girls at the edge of adolescence.

Education is the time-honored, nonviolent means of social change, the alternative to revolution. And education at present in this country is largely in the hands of women, who as mothers, teachers, and therapists are directly in contact with people's desires for relationship and for knowledge and therefore in touch with the resistance. Perhaps women are currently in a position to constitute an Outsiders' Society.

The old question stirs: What if women . . . irrepressible question! Half the population in every generation. Could women, as Madeline Grumet envisions, turn the practice of teaching—a relational practice like mothering and psychotherapy—from "women's work" into "the work of women," so that instead of leading what Grumet calls "the great escape" from the daily rhythms of the maternal order to the clock time of the paternal state,[37] women would institute a new order (using private means in private as Woolf would have it) by teaching a different knowledge and creating a different practice of human relationships?

At the beginning of the second act of *Lysistrata*, Lysistrata despairs; the women are leaving the Acropolis and rushing home to their husbands. "I know you miss your husbands," she says, "but don't you realize that they miss you as well? . . . Be strong sisters," she enjoins the women. "There is an oracle that we will triumph if only we don't fall out among ourselves."[38]

Sara Ruddick heals what is a major division within and among women—the division between mother and resister—by defining a women's politics of resistance that is relationally rather than heroically conceived. This practice of resistance is rooted in the body (its vulnerability, its promise, its power). It is a practice of "preservative love." Ruddick takes her cue from the Madres of Argentina and the women of Chile, describing a strategy that draws its imperative in the singularity of human beings and the irreplaceability of human relationships, rather than in visions of immortality or superhuman strength. If only women would make a shift within their existing practice as mothers, separating out those elements that support militarism (the worshipping of martyrs and heros) from those that subvert it (women's irreverent language of loyalty, love, and outrage), women could move readily, Ruddick suspects, "from denial to truthfulness, from parochialism to solidarity, from inauthenticity to active responsibility."[39] In short, women could move from psychological to political resistance.

Central to this journey is a recovery of anger as the political emotion par excellence—the bellwether of oppression, injustice, bad treatment; the clue that something is wrong in the relational surround (a fin on the horizon, a sudden darkening, a bad shadow). Teresa Bernardez, writing about women and anger from the two-culture vantage point of an Argentinean-born, North American psychotherapist, reminds her readers that cultural injunctions against anger in women turn into psychological inhibitions that "prevent rebellious acts," with the result that women become complicit in women's silence and isolation. The process of psychotherapy then involves a kind of reverse alchemy, whereby anger that has soured into bitterness and hatred becomes once again simply anger—"the conscious response to an awareness of injustices suffered or losses and grievances sustained . . . [the anger] which involves self-love and awareness of the responsibility of making choices."[40] Like 11-year-old Sarah's anger that lives in the daylight of her relationships, or Tessie's anger that sits comfortably side-by-side with self-love. Bernardez observes that when people are living under conditions of political oppression or terror, they often come not to know what they know and "have forgotten what they have forgotten." She also observes that anger silenced "contributes to the making of depression." And depression in women tends to begin at adolescence.

Perhaps women have forgotten girls. And not remembered this dissociation or disconnection between women and girls at adolescence. So that relationships between adolescent girls and women hold a key to the psychology and the politics of women's resistance.

When Anjli brought her paper on "To His Coy Mistress" to her English teacher, Mrs. Franklin, Nancy Franklin realized that she was hearing the poem in a way she had not heard it before—very differently from the way she had learned to listen in the course of her graduate training. Anjli had been asked to analyze the poem for tone; she was taking an advanced class taught simultaneously at several schools in the area. Nancy Franklin is one of the women pursuing the question, What does it mean to be a woman teaching girls? It is to this group of women, in the third year of their meeting, that she speaks about Anjli's paper and her decision to join Anjli's resistance.

Anjli, in the midst of writing her analysis—listening to the tone of the poem in her house late at night—suddenly begins writing in the first person as she takes in what she is hearing: the voice of an older man bent on overcoming a young woman's resistance ("Had we but world enough, and time, / This coyness, Lady, were no crime"). And Nancy Franklin, taking in Anjli's voice, feels the power of the poem anew and also the force of what Anjli is hearing. Anjli writes, her teacher recalls, "I am writing this paper and it is late at night, and I am terrified because this is such a morbid poem ("Thy beauty shall no more be found, / Nor, in thy marble vault, shall sound / My echoing song: then worms shall try / That long preserved virginity, / And your quaint honor turn to dust, / And into ashes all my lust"). This is such a frightening poem."

Anjli's paper was submitted to six teachers for cross-grading exercises, designed to ensure consistency of standards. One woman, Franklin recalls, "actually wrote on the paper: 'She doesn't understand *carpe diem.* Why doesn't she know this term? This is not a college level paper.'" Another wrote, "She misreads Marvell's playfulness." And yet—Nancy Franklin says, caught momentarily by the standards of her colleagues and then resisting their disconnection from Anjli and their dismissal of her reading—"this paper was beautiful, and it made me see the poem in a new way." Sustaining this connection, she draws out its implications for Anjli, for herself, and also for society:

> This is a young girl; this is a 17-year-old, very innocent but very bright girl. Reading this, Lord knows, you go back and read that poem, at two o'clock in the morning. And she was terrified—the voice of an older man speaking to a young girl. And the comments she got on this paper. They all said: C-, you know, no good. "Doesn't know stanzaic patterns, missed all this playfulness, and *carpe diem*, *carpe diem.*" Now there's the

> educational system at work. What did it tell her? Go underground; to survive, go underground, at least until you get out of this system. Or worse.[41]

Anjli read the graders' comments, discussed them with her teacher, remembered hearing about *carpe diem*, reread the poem, and, Nancy Franklin writes, "found that indeed she could see the poem that way but more importantly, she could see it both ways." She knows that "she could rewrite the paper now that she understands the way she was supposed to react, saying what she is supposed to say . . . 'If you were a guy,' she says, smiling, 'It might be really funny.'" But Anjli also still cringes at the poem's morbid images: "I don't think," she concludes, "a class full of girls could really laugh at this."[42] What is puzzling then, given Anjli's perspective, and also potentially treacherous, is the position of the women graders; Anjli assumes that she will be understood by girls, but she cannot assume such understanding from women.

At the intersection between political resistance and psychological resistance, at the time of adolescence, girls' psychological development becomes indelibly political. If girls know what they know and bring themselves into relationship, they will be in conflict with prevailing authorities. If girls do not know what they know and take themselves out of relationship, they will be in trouble with themselves. The ability of girls to tell it from both sides and to see it both ways is not an illustration of relativism (the abandonment of an absolute truth) but rather a demonstration of girls' understanding of relationship raised to a cultural level and a provisional solution to a difficult problem of relationship: how to stay connected with themselves and with others, how to keep in touch with themselves and with the world.

As 11-year-old Tessie underscores the importance of voicing her argument with her mother, so Anjli voices the disparity between how she reacts and how she is supposed to react, what she says and what she is supposed to say, according to the authorities who correct and grade her. And Tessie's openness, at least in theory, to her friend's hearing her mother's voice differently from the way she does, corresponds to Anjli's generosity toward those who hear the poem differently: the guys and the graders. Women teaching girls, then, are faced with a series of intricate problems of relationship. Girls must learn the traditions that frame and structure the world they are entering, and they also must hold on to their own ways of hearing and seeing. How can women stay with girls and also teach cultural traditions? How can girls stay with women and also with themselves? What can women teach girls about living in a world that is still governed by men?

"What happens to girls when they get to that age?" Sharon Miller asks. A teacher of 12-year-olds and the mother of a 12-year-old daughter, she returns to what has been the riddle of female development—to Freud's question and the question posed by women therapists across the century: Why is it that girls, who seem "more intelligent and livelier than boys of the same age, [who] go out more to meet the external world and at the same time form stronger [connections with people]," seem to become less intelligent and less lively when they reach adolescence?[43] Freud observes that "the constitution will not adapt itself to its function without a struggle," and then goes on to talk about the function of women. Our research on girls' development has focused on elucidating the struggle, which is readily observed in girls at the time of adolescence.

Like girls in novels and poems written by women,[44] girls interviewed in contemporary school settings speak about taking themselves out of relationship as they approach adolescence: about "building a little shield," about "getting afraid to say when you're mad at somebody," about "losing confidence in myself. I was losing track of myself, really, and losing the kind of person I was."[45] Paradoxically, girls are taking themselves out of relationship for the sake of relationship and self-consciously letting go of themselves. This doubling of the psychological language augments the confusion girls experience at this time—the inability in a way to say what is happening because the very words "self" and "relationship" have doubled in meaning, as if one psychology has been superimposed on another, causing girls to lose track of their own experience as they move into the larger world.[46]

Lyn Brown, analyzing girls' narratives of relationship, notes that as girls approach adolescence they tend to withdraw authorization from their own experience and to replace realistic with inauthentic or idealized descriptions of relationships. Perhaps for this reason, girls who are developing well according to standard psychological measures and cultural yardsticks are also

> engaging in difficult and sometimes painful personal battles around issues of voice and authorization, unsure of the accuracy of their own perceptions, afraid that speaking up will damage relationships or compromise their image in the eyes of others . . . showing signs of an impasse in their ability to act in the face of conflict.[47]

What happens to girls when they reach this age? "I think," Sharon Miller says, "they have let go of themselves. I think it is the unusual middle school girl who can say . . . if you don't like me the way I am, fine. Most girls can't say that because there is no one there." Why not? I ask her. I am thinking of the girls who are so resolute, so present at age 11. "Well, that's the question, you know; what happens to girls when they get to that age? Well, because that is the age when girls start identifying with adult women." And then, suddenly, seeing the circle closing, she says, hand rising, covering her mouth, "My God," as tears begin flowing, "And there is nothing there."[48]

Like a film running backwards, women teaching girls arrive at the moments of our own resistance and come up against our own solutions to the problems of relationship that girls face. Then women may encounter our own reluctance to know what they know and come to the realization that such knowledge is contained in our bodies; and they may discover that we have succumbed to the temptation to model perfection by trying to be perfect role-models for girls and thus have taken ourselves out of relationship with girls—in part to hide our imperfection, but also perhaps to keep girls from feeling our sadness and our anger. Women teaching girls, however, also may discover that we are harboring, within ourselves, a girl who lives in her body, who is insistent on speaking, who intensely desires relationships and knowledge, and who, perhaps at the time of adolescence, went underground or was overwhelmed. It may be that adolescent girls are looking for this girl in women, and feeling her absence or her hidden presence. And it may be that women, in the name of being good women, have been modeling for girls her repudiation—teaching girls the necessity of a loss or renunciation, which girls question.

Perhaps there is a new cycle that, once beginning, will break up an old impasse in women's development and affect men as well. If women and girls can stay with one another at the time when girls reach adolescence, girls' playfulness and irreverence may tap the wellsprings of women's resistance. And women, in turn, taking in girls' embodiment, their outspokenness, and their courage may encourage girls' desire for relationship and for knowledge and teach girls that they can say what they know and not be left all alone.

Coda:

"Dear Kitty," Anne Frank writes on January 6, 1944, at the age of 14, in a passage from her diary that her father edited—in exactly the manner she predicts in the passage:

> I have three things to confess to you today. . . . I *must* tell someone, and you are the best to tell, as I know that come what may you always keep a secret. . . . You know that I've grumbled a lot about Mummy, yet still tried to be nice to her again. Now it is suddenly clear to me what she lacks. Mummy herself has told us that she looked upon us more as her friends than her daughters; now that is all very fine of course, but still a friend can't take a mother's place. *I need my mother as an example which I can follow. I want to be able to respect her and though my mother is an example to me in most things she is precisely the kind of example that I do not want to follow.* I have the feeling that Margot thinks differently about these things and would never be able to understand what I've just told you. And Daddy avoids all arguments about Mummy. [deleted passage is italicized][49]

"*One Conclusion*," Emma writes, beginning a new page in her journal,

> One of the conclusions I come to is that many/most of the paintings/statues/artwork of women I have seen are of women

> naked. A lot of the art of women that I saw was done by men. Maybe because the women posed. None of the girls I saw were naked. Maybe because artists like to have people pose naked, and they think women are better because they have more growth.

One question, Malka writes at the end of her second conversation with the Queen of Babylon, "Did these people, places, painted, sculpted, did they live? Did they live in the heart of the painter, sculptor?"

"Wouldn't there have been," Anna says irreverently—she has just finished writing a paper about the Church and Galileo—"Wouldn't there have been a lot of animal stuff on Noah's ark after forty days?"

"I think I am trying," Rosie says, "to attach value to things. This is important. This is not important. Maybe order things more." What do you order them to, I ask, wondering what key she is tuning to, what standard she has in mind. And Rosie, the embodied saint, the underground woman, suddenly turns philosophical:

> I don't know . . . but I guess I know that there should be an order, and I was trying to decide what that order was. Maybe that is part of what I am looking for . . . is an order to my life. This is getting deep, philosophical.

I am listening to girls' questions—following girls' inquiry into relationships as it becomes more philosophical, more critical, and also more psychologically and politically dangerous. Emma's curiosity is edging toward men's feelings about women's bodies; Malka begins to trace the channels connecting men's hearts with cultural icons. If this inquiry continues, girls will find the line that connects the personal and the political, the line between the psychology of men and the cultural framework, and wonder how they fit in.

"I don't know," Rosie says, Socrates' plaint. "I guess I know," she follows, in rapid succession. She is observing how her mother spends her life, her time, asking in effect the same question that Malka asks the Queen of Babylon: "What are you doing?" And seeing what her mother has to say—whether her mother might come up with the Queen's funny answer: "Brushing my hair. I was interrupted this morning by a revolt," the answer that captures the doubling of women's lives and also speaks to girls' questions about what gives women pleasure and what women value.

Rosie, the sharp-eyed adolescent, notices that her mother's "small study and bedroom are messy." She will have to create her own order of living, find some way to orchestrate her life. "I don't know . . . I know . . . you know . . . do you know? . . ." voices of the underground, speaking under the sign of repression, marking dissociations that are still tenuous, knowledge that is fragile, reaching out for connections that can sustain the promise that a secret underground one day will become a public resistance. Then a healthy resistance that is evident in girls at adolescence, rather than turning inward and becoming psychologically corrosive, can stay in the open air of relationships. And by remaining political, work to bring a new order of living into the world.

ENDNOTES

[1]The quotations from the 11-year-old girls are taken from the girls' journals and also from my journal. The Theater, Writing and Outing Club is part of a prevention project, "Strengthening Healthy Resistance and Courage in Girls," conducted by Annie Rogers, Normi Noel, and myself in public and private schools in the Boston area. The project centers on developing girls' voices at a time when they tend to be strong and creating authentic or resonant relationships between women and girls. This research has been encouraged and made possible by the support of Joan Lipsitz and the Lilly Endowment; Steven Minter and the Cleveland Foundation; Lawrence Cremin, Marion Faldet, and Linda Fitzgerald of the Spencer Foundation; Judith Simpson and the Gund Foundation; Benjamin Barber and the Walt Whitman Center for Democracy at Rutgers University; the American Association of University Women; Patricia Albjerg Graham, Dean of the Harvard Graduate School of Education; Virginia Kahn, Founder of the Atrium School; and Leah Rhys, Head of Laurel School.

[2] Sigmund Freud, "The Interpretation of Dreams," 1899/1900. Vols. 4 and 5 of *The Standard Edition of the Complete Psychological Works of Sigmund Freud* (London: Hogarth Press, 1953). See also *The Complete Letters of Sigmund Freud to Wilhelm Fleiss: 1887–1904* (Cambridge, MA: Harvard University Press, 1985).

[3] Carol Gilligan, *In a Different Voice: Psychological Theory and Women's Development* (Cambridge, MA.: Harvard University Press, 1982); "Prologue" and "Teaching Shakespeare's Sister: Notes from the Underground of Female Adolescence." In Gilligan, Lyons, & Hanmer (Eds.), *Making Connections* (Cambridge, MA: Harvard University Press, 1990); Carol Gilligan, Lyn Mikel Brown, and Annie Rogers, "Psyche Embedded: A Place for Body, Relationships and Culture in Personality Theory." In A.I. Rabin, R. Zucker, R. Emmons, & S. Frank (Eds.), *Studying Persons and Lives* (New York: Springer, 1990).

[4] Virginia Woolf, *Three Guineas* (San Diego: Harcourt Brace Jovanovich, 1938), p. 6.

[5] *The Diary of Anne Frank: The Critical Edition* (New York: Doubleday, 1989), p. 678.

[6]Aristophanes, *Lysistrata/The Acharnians/The Clouds* (London: Penguin Books, 1973), pp. 180–181.

[7] Nathaniel Hawthorne, *The Scarlet Letter* (New York: Modern Library, 1950 [1850]), pp. 299, 184.

[8] *Ibid.*, p. 178.

[9] *Ibid.*, p. 184.

[10]*Ibid.*, pp. 187–188.

[11] Sigmund Freud,"The Case of Fräulein Elisabeth von R.," from Joseph Breuer and Sigmund Freud, *Studies on Hysteria* 1893–95. Vol. 2 of *The Standard Edition*, p. 161. See also Elaine Showalter, *The Female Malady* (New York: Penguin Books, 1985).

[12] Hawthorne, *op. cit.*, p. 227.

[13] *Ibid.*, pp. 299.

[14] Claudia Koonz, *Mothers in the Fatherland* (New York: St. Martin's Press, 1986), pp. 310, 332.

[15] Diana E. H. Russell, *Lives of Courage: Women for a New South Africa* (New York: Basic Books, 1989), p. 24.

[16] *Ibid.*

[17] Woolf, *op. cit.*, p. 143.

[18] *Ibid.*, p. 93.

[19] *Ibid.*, p. 142.

[20] Shawn Slovo, *A World Apart* (London: Faber and Faber, 1988), p. x.

[21] *Ibid.*, p. ix.

[22] *Ibid.*, p. 107.

[23] *Ibid.*, pp. xi, 18.

[24] These psychological truths seem to me self-evident—picked up by writers and identified by psychologists with a good ear for the relational world. For example, the power of the unspoken is mentioned both by Freud and by Shakespeare; in *Macbeth*, Malcolm says to Macduff, "Give sorrow words. The grief that does not speak/Whispers the o'erfraught heart and bids it break."

[25] Anna's quotations are taken from interviews conducted over the course of a five-year study of girls' development at the Laurel School in Cleveland, Ohio. Papers from the project, which involved girls and women who were diverse in racial as well as economic background, were presented at the Harvard-Laurel Conference on "The Psychology of Women and the Education of Girls," held in Cleveland, April 1990.

[26] Tessie was one of ten 11-year-old girls living in a suburb of Boston and interviewed by Sharry Langdale in 1981 as part of the Project on the Psychology of Women and the Development of Girls conducted at Harvard University.

[27] This analysis was carried out by Lisa Marie Kulpinski, a graduate student in the Human Development and Psychology Program at Harvard University, and reported in her paper, "Adolescence: Hitting a Fork in the Road," 1990.

[28] Frank, *op. cit.*, p. 545.

[29] Glen Elder and Avshalom Caspi, "Studying Lives in a Changing Society: Sociological and Personological Explorations." In A. Rabin, R. Zucker, R. Emmons, & S. Frank (Eds.), *Studying Persons and Lives* (New York: Springer, 1990), pp. 226–228. See also Anne Peterson, "Adolescent Development" (*Annual Review of Psychology*, 39, pp. 583–607, 1988).

[30] Woolf, *op. cit.*, p. 113.

[31] Jorie Graham, *Erosion* (Princeton: Princeton University Press, 1983), pp. 16–21.

[32] Toni Morrison, *The Bluest Eye*. (New York: Pocket Books, 1970), p. 53.

[33] Frank, *op. cit.*, p. 557.

[34] Sophocles, *Oedipus the King*. In the more literal Loeb Classics translation, this line reads "How could the soil thy father eared so long / Endure to bear in silence such a wrong" (Cambridge, MA: Harvard

University Press, 1912), p. 113. In the text, for purposes of clarity, I have cited Fitzgerald's freer translation.

[35] Lyn Mikel Brown, my companion on this journey, was the research director of the Harvard-Laurel Project.

[36] Dianne Argyris and Judy Dorney, graduate students in the Human Development and Psychology Program at Harvard University, compiled and analyzed the girls' thoughts and feelings about the Laurel School honor code, and this work was the basis for the presentation to the faculty.

[37] Madeline R. Grumet, *Bitter Milk: Women and Teaching* (Amherst: University of Massachusetts Press, 1988), pp. 58, 25. See also Jane Roland Martin, *Reclaiming a Conversation* (New Haven: Yale University Press, 1985), and Mary Belenky, Blythe Clinchy, Nancy Goldberger, & Jill Tarule, *Women's Ways of Knowing: The Development of Self, Voice, and Mind* (New York: Basic Books, 1986).

[38] Aristophanes, *op. cit.*, p. 212.

[39] Sara Ruddick, *Maternal Thinking: Toward a Politics of Peace* (Boston: Beacon Press, 1989), pp. 227–230.

[40] Teresa Bernardez, "Women and Anger: Cultural Prohibitions and the Feminine Ideal" (Wellesley College: Stone Center Working Paper Series, *31*, 1988), p. 5. See also Jean Baker Miller, *Toward a New Psychology of Women* (Boston: Beacon Press, 1976) for a discussion of women and anger and the roots of anger in women's political oppression.

[41] Quotations taken from the taped transcript of the Women Teaching Girls project, Harvard-Laurel retreat, February 1990. The retreats, which brought together psychologists and teachers, and crossed the educational span from nursery to university, were designed and led by Judy Dorney. For a description of the retreat process see Judy Dorney, "Women Teaching Girls: Relationships in the Practice of Teaching" (1990), a working paper of the Harvard Project on the Psychology of Women and the Development of Girls. See also note 35.

[42] Nancy S. Franklin, "Teachers' Tales of Empowerment: A Story from an English Teacher," a paper presented at the Harvard-Laurel Conference on "The Psychology of Women and The Education of Girls," April 6, 1990, Cleveland, Ohio.

[43] Freud, "Femininity," Lecture XXXIII, *New Introductory Lectures on Psycho-Analysis* (1933 [1932]), Vol. 22 of *The Standard Edition*), p. 117, and also "The Transformations of Puberty" in *Three Essays on the Theory of Sexuality* (1905), Vol. 7. See also Karen Horney, "The Flight

from Womanhood" (*International Journal of Psycho-analysis*, *7*, pp. 324–339, 1926); Clara M. Thompson, "Adolescence" and other papers in *Interpersonal Psychoanalysis* (New York: Basic Books, 1964); and Jean Baker Miller, "The Development of Women's Sense of Self," (Wellesley College: Stone Center Working Paper Series, *12*, 1984).

[44] See for example, Charlotte Brontë, *Jane Eyre*; Toni Morrison, *The Bluest Eye*; Jamaica Kincaid, *Annie John*; Carson McCullers, *The Member of the Wedding*; Margaret Atwood, *Cat's Eye*; Michelle Cliff, "Claiming an Identity They Taught Me to Despise," in *The Land of Look Behind*; and Sharon Olds, "Time-Travel," in *Satan Says*.

[45] Lyn Mikel Brown, "A Problem of Vision: The Development of Relational Voice in Girls Ages 7 to 16" (*Women's Studies Quarterly*, *19*(1/2), pp. 52–71, 1991). See also Lyn Mikel Brown, *Narratives of Relationship: The Development of a Care Voice in Girls Ages 7 to 16* (Unpublished Ed.D. Dissertation, Harvard University Graduate School of Education, 1989).

[46] For a fuller discussion of this phenomenon, see Gilligan, *In a Different Voice* and "Teaching Shakespeare's Sister," and also Lori Stern, *Disavowing the Self in Female Adolescence: A Case Study Analysis* (Unpublished Ed.D. Dissertation, Harvard University Graduate School of Education, 1990).

[47] Lyn Mikel Brown and Carol Gilligan, "The Psychology of Women and the Development of Girls." This paper, originally presented at the Harvard-Laurel Conference on The Psychology of Women and the Education of Girls, April 5, 1990, Cleveland, Ohio, will be published in *Feminism and Psychology*.

[48] Quotations taken from the taped transcript of the Women Teaching Girls Project, Harvard-Laurel Retreat, October 1989.

[49] Frank, *op. cit.*, p. 440.

REFERENCES

Aristophanes. (1973). *Lysistrata/ The Acharnians/ The Clouds*. London: Penguin Books.

Atwood, M. (1988). *Cat's eye*. New York: Doubleday.

Belenky, M., Clinchy, B., Goldberger, N., & Tarule, J. (1986). *Women's ways of knowing: The development of self, voice, and mind*. New York: Basic Books.

Bernardez, R. (1988). Women and anger: Cultural prohibitions and the feminine ideal. *Work in Progress, No. 31*. Wellesley, MA: Stone Center Working Papers Series.

Breuer, J., & Freud, S. (1955). Studies on hysteria. 1893–95. (Case Histories: The case of Fräulein Elisabeth von R.). In J. Strachey (Ed. and Trans.), *The standard edition of the complete psychological works of Sigmund Freud* (Vol. 2, pp. 135–181). London: Hogarth Press.

Brontë, C. (1966). *Jane Eyre*. Harmondsworth, Middlesex: Penguin.

Brown, L. (1989). *Narratives of relationship: The development of a care voice in girls ages 7 to 16*. Unpublished doctoral dissertation, Harvard University Graduate School of Education, Cambridge, MA.

Brown, L. (1991). A problem of vision: The development of voice and relational knowledge in girls ages 7 to 16. *Women's Studies Quarterly, 19*(1/2), 52–71.

Brown, L., & Gilligan, C. (1993). Meeting at the crossroads: Women's psychology and girls' development. *Feminism and Psychology, 3* (1), 11–35.

Cliff, M. (1985). *The Land of look behind*. Ithaca, NY: Firebrand Books.

Elder, G., & Caspi, A. (1990). Studying lives in a changing society: Sociological and personological explorations. In A. Rabin, R. Zucker, R. Emmons, & S. Frank (Eds.), *Studying persons and lives*. New York: Springer.

Frank, A. (1989). *The diary of Anne Frank: The critical edition*. New York: Doubleday.

Franklin, N. (1990, April). Teachers' tales of empowerment: A story from an English teacher. Paper presented at the Harvard-Laurel Conference on The Psychology of Women and the Education of Girls, Cleveland, OH.

Freud, S. (1964). New introductory lectures on psychoanalysis (Lecture XXXIII: Femininity). In J. Strachey (Ed. and Trans.), *The standard edition of the complete psychological works of Sigmund Freud* (Vol. 22, pp. 112–135). London: Hogarth Press.

Freud, S. (1953). The interpretation of dreams. 1899/1900. In J. Strachey (Ed. and Trans.), *The standard edition of the complete psychological works of Sigmund Freud* (Vols. 4 and 5). London: Hogarth Press.

Freud, S. (1953). Three essays on the theory of sexuality (The transformations of puberty). In J. Strachey (Ed. and Trans.), *The standard edition of the complete psychological works of Sigmund Freud* (Vol. 7, pp. 207–230). London: Hogarth Press.

Freud, S. (1985). *The complete letters of Sigmund Freud to Wilhelm Fleiss, 1887–1904* (J. Moussaieff Masson, Trans.). Cambridge, MA: Belknap Press of Harvard University Press.

Gilligan, C. (1982). *In a different voice: Psychological theory and women's development.* Cambridge, MA: Harvard University Press.

Gilligan, C. (1990). Teaching Shakespeare's sister: Notes from the underground of female adolescence. In C. Gilligan, N. Lyons, & T. Hanmer (Eds.), *Making connections: The relational worlds of adolescent girls at Emma Willard School* (pp. 6–29). Cambridge, MA: Harvard University Press.

Gilligan, C., Brown, L., & Rogers, A. (1990). Psyche embedded: A place for body, relationships, and culture in personality theory. In A. Rabin, R. Zucker, R. Emmons, & S. Frank (Eds.), *Studying persons and lives.* New York: Springer.

Gilligan, C., Lyons, N., and Hanmer, T. (Eds.). (1990). *Making connections: The relational worlds of adolescent girls at Emma Willard School.* Cambridge, MA: Harvard University Press.

Graham, J. (1983). *Erosion.* Princeton: Princeton University Press.

Grumet, M. (1988). *Bitter milk: Women and teaching.* Amherst: University of Massachusetts Press.

Hawthorne, N. (1950). *The scarlet letter.* New York: Modern Library. (Original work published 1850)

Horney, K. (1926). The flight from womanhood. *International Journal of Psycho-analysis,* 7, 324–339.

Kincaid, J. (1985). *Annie John.* New York: Farrar, Straus & Giroux.

Koonz, C. (1986). *Mothers in the fatherland.* New York: St. Martin's Press.

Kulpinski, L. (1990). Adolescence: Hitting a fork in the road. Unpublished paper, Harvard University Graduate School of Education, Cambridge, MA.

Martin, J. (1985). *Reclaiming a conversation.* New Haven: Yale University Press.

McCullers, C. (1973). *The member of the wedding.* New York: Bantam. (Original work published 1946)

Miller, J. (1976). *Toward a new psychology of women.* Boston: Beacon.

Miller, J. (1984). The development of women's sense of self. *Work in Progress, No. 12.* Wellesley, MA: Stone Center Working Papers Series.

Morrison, T. (1970). *The bluest eye.* New York: Pocket Books.

Olds, S. (1980). *Satan says.* Pittsburgh: University of Pittsburgh Press.

Peterson, A. (1988). Adolescent development. *Annual Review of Psychology,* 39, 226–228.

Ruddick, S. (1989). *Maternal thinking: Toward a politics of peace*. Boston: Beacon.

Russell, D. (1989). *Lives of courage: Women for a new South Africa*. New York: Basic Books.

Showalter, E. (1985). *The female malady*. New York: Penguin Books.

Slovo, S. (1988). *A world apart*. London: Faber and Faber.

Sophocles. (1912). *Oedipus the king*: Loeb Classical Library (F. Storr, Trans.). Cambridge, MA: Harvard University Press.

Sophocles. (1949). *Oedipus Rex: An English version* (D. Fitts & R. Fitzgerald, Trans.). New York: Harcourt, Brace & Co.

Stern, L. (1990). *Disavowing the self in female adolescence: A case study analysis*. Unpublished doctoral dissertation, Harvard University Graduate School of Education, Cambridge, MA.

Thompson, C. (1964). *Interpersonal psychoanalysis*. New York: Basic Books.

Woolf, V. (1966). *Three guineas*. San Diego: Harcourt Brace Jovanovich. (Original work published 1938)

8

Discussion of the Papers by Jean Baker Miller and Carol Gilligan

SILVIA W. OLARTE, M.D.

The Miller and Gilligan papers are a reflection of a long and productive effort to challenge old ways of thinking about the psychology of women. Their work, which has evolved from the pioneering and courageous work of innovative thinkers like Karen Horney, has influenced a whole generation of professionals in the fields of health science, psychology, education, and law. Dr. Miller and Dr. Gilligan have been able to question and revise seminal controversial formulations, while creating new parameters through which we can continue our understanding of the vicissitudes of women's psychological development within a societal frame of reference that is patriarchal, hierarchical, and controlling of the sources of power.

In my professional life their work has been crucial to my understanding and successful resolution of the complexity in women's ever-present desire and struggle to integrate their evolving self within the context of relationships.

Dr. Miller spoke to us about the central psychological formative role of a sense of connection to others in women's development. Developmentally, women's sense of self and of worth is based in their ability to maintain and make relationships. Women endow life activities arising within a context of relationships, with a sense of value and effectiveness that fosters in them a greater sense of connection rather than a sense of separation, a state thought to be the one to strive for by both the mature male and the mature female.

For the most part, the woman's role entails the active participation in the development of other people. Within the context of mutually enhancing relationships, this complex activity comprises engaging with another person in such a manner as to secure the psychological development of both people involved in the interaction.

Dr. Miller reminds us that as we have not had a societal situation based on the search for full mutuality, we have not had psychological developmental theories based on relationships that foster mutual development through childhood and adult life, nor have we had an abundance of mutually enhancing relationships. The key ingredient to allow for mutual growth is to be able to respond empathically to each other, to provide an initial connection with each other so as to allow for further clarification of each other's own feelings and thoughts. The further development of both experiences within the context of the caring relationship makes the individuals feel stronger and more knowledgeable about themselves. They now feel empowered to act beyond this initial empathic response toward the outside world. Their enhanced sense of self-worth facilitates their ability to communicate with others, thus fostering further connections.

Relationships that foster mutual development through childhood and adult life are based on allowing children to experience and explore within their formative relationships the full gamut of their feelings and thoughts toward enhancing their understanding. This exploration need not be curtailed by the authority's desire to bring the child to conform within specific rules. In spite of difference in knowledge or experience, the relationship would permit for mutual exploration of the experience, feeling, or thought. Through this process of mutual understanding and growth, individuals will not need to ignore parts of their selves to procure a relationship.

Besides, a child who learns how to handle uncomfortable feelings-thoughts evoked by life experiences within the frame of reference of mutually enhancing relationships will be able to provide such experience to others when later on these others require such empathic understanding from him or her.

Disconnections happen, Dr. Miller tells us, when adults or children are deprived of participating in mutually enhancing, mutually responsive relationships. One participant learns that his or her particular experience cannot be shared. Sharing threatens the relationship. To protect the relationship, the individual learns to ward off parts of herself or himself.

Dr. Miller and Dr. Gilligan have presented us with examples of disconnections in relationships through the voice of adolescent girls in their incipient understanding of their relationship with the society at large, and as related by clients in our clinical practices when they try to integrate their desire for relatedness and the validity of their inner selves.

Emotions we share in our desire to be empathetically understood can evoke uncomfortable feelings in others. In order to protect themselves from those feelings, they can dismiss us, reject us, or devalue us, as in the example between Ann and Tom. Their lack of empathy leaves us still experiencing our initial overwhelming emotions for which we solicited empathy, plus anger about their response to us, and confusion about our own experience. This confusion fosters doubt about our self-worth. We tend to blame ourselves and not to question others' inability to empathize.

To not devalue ourselves we must first learn to recognize our initial response to others' lack of empathy for our experience, that is, to recognize our disappointment or even anger at their inability to hear us, to disagree with or to oppose us while allowing for the relationship to continue.

But to be able, as women, to validate our own perception, Dr. Gilligan reminds us, we would have had to be allowed in our adolescence to know what we knew and to have been respected in our willingness to be outspoken.

What we begin to know in adolescence is the power of our bodies, our desires, our feelings. The person we feel we are becoming is not who society wishes us to become. Dr. Gilligan alerts us that we learn to share and to present our feelings-thoughts only to ourselves in the intimacy of our diaries, or in the safety of specific intimate relationships, the "best friends," Ann and Beth, that with the passage of time have permitted us to trust their ability to provide us with mutually enhancing relationships.

To comply with the given social order—defined by men, based on the study of male subjects and extrapolated then to women—women have had, at some point in their development, to deny what they know about themselves or adapt this knowledge to the prevailing definition of their gender. Dr. Gilligan's research shows us that what is normal for a girl, to speak up, to be different, to show anger, to fight, to express bad as well as good thoughts and feelings, becomes treacherous for the adolescent girl, a sign of danger, of not being chosen.

It is during adolescence, Dr. Gilligan explains, that girls have to face the conflict of holding on to what they know, bring themselves and this knowledge into relationships, and alienate authority, or to deny what they know about themselves, take themselves out of relationships, and be in trouble with themselves. Dr. Gilligan's research describes girls' ability to see both sides of an argument. This ability of girls to tell it from both sides expresses a creative solution to the problem of how to stay connected to themselves and others, how to keep in touch with what they know and with the world as they must know it, how to bridge this paradox-maintaining communication within a relationship versus defining a lack of moral maturity.

Both Dr. Gilligan and Dr. Miller remind us that women are the ones who actively participate in the development of other people, not only in their gender role of mothers and caretakers, but in their overrepresented numbers among formative careers such as teachers.

As of now, and as long as a male-oriented power order prevails, the formative relationship between women and girls is defined in conflict, as women try to help girls to hold on to what they know about themselves while teaching them to comply with cultural traditions. To the degree that women have voiced their discontent with the traditional male-oriented power system, they have experienced alienation from relationships and isolation from others.

Instead of continuing to close aspects of themselves to try to fit into the idealized image of the female in a male-oriented hierarchical social structure, women can foster among themselves and with the girls they are developing, mutually enhancing relationships to explore their common predicament, their emotions, feelings, and experiences in order to enhance their understanding of themselves. These women will not then tend to doubt their knowledge, experience, feelings, or thoughts when engaged in disconnected interpersonal experiences with anyone representing authority and power. Instead, they will be able to hold on to who they are and what they know and define their needs or wants in such a manner that a potentially disconnected relationship with the other might be transformed into a mutually enhancing relationship.

9

Discussion of the Papers by Jean Baker Miller and Carol Gilligan

MARIO RENDON, M.D.

GENDER AND BEING: TWO PSYCHOANALYTIC VIEWPOINTS

I heard someone say, years ago, that in one of the famous Catholic Church Councils, perhaps in the Middle Ages, the agenda was to discuss whether women, like men, had a soul. Today, after the remarkable achievements of patriarchal civilization—among which are the amputation and dismembering of mother earth, we may ask the inverted question: Do men, like women, have a soul?

Of course, the soul was ineffable and could not be studied. We had to rename it "psyche" to do so. Many years after the Council, from a new brand of dialectical psychology—psychoanalysis Freud would come up with a self-proclaimed scientific answer to the question: the woman's soul is a lesser version of the man's. One woman disciple of Freud spoke up against this unfair and discriminatory answer: Karen Horney.

I would like to draw some comparisons between the Freudian and the Horneyian theories of psychoanalysis, with the central issue of gender in mind. I will thus make an effort to complement the viewpoints of the other contributors to this volume, particularly the ideas of Jean Baker Miller and Carol Gilligan. The main question I will try to answer is, How is the female gender reflected in the theories of Sigmund Freud and Karen Horney?

There is no question that Freud, as the founder of psychoanalysis, made a major contribution to humanity; this was recognized by Horney. However, as Horney and others point out, Freud's theory is phallocentric and patriarchal. This is abundantly documented in the literature. We may underline, however, that in his struggle between loyalty to neurology and medicine, and the fact that his clinical findings could not be explained by these disciplines, Freud, although clearly begging help from psychology, never was able to give up his biologism. He was always hopeful that bioscience would ultimately corroborate and legitimize his findings. The most clear example of this conflict is reflected in his "Project for a Scientific Psychology for Neurologists," where he attempted to frame psychological discoveries, already quite coherent in meaning, into the procrustean bed of neurology. Freud's loyalty extended to the methodology used by medicine and the physical sciences, which was the prevalent analytical methodology of Descartes. In summary, Freud's ultimate beginning, as you know, was the energy represented by drives that were presumably active, masculine, and best represented by the phallic symbol, the symbol of libidinal energy.

In this regard, Horney's rebellion was initially aimed at this "given" of Freud, what I have called his ultimate beginning. In a series of tentative approximations, reflected in her *Feminine Psychology* (see Horney, 1967/1973), Horney clearly challenged the phallocentric theory of Freud, the primacy of masculine libido, and the relegation of women to a position of natural deviance. Horney struggled with these issues, and after several failed attempts to mend Freud's theory to better fit her own observations, she realized that her total scientific expression was being obliterated by her own loyalty and that a break with Freud was necessary. As we all know, she was forced out of the psychoanalytic mainstream and stripped of her academic status.

One of Horney's main criticisms of Freud was his excessive biologism. Of course, invoking biology is almost like invoking God. Being-in-itself, impenetrable, and governed by its own laws, we have to accept nature's inscrutable law. Today, we still hear phallocentric ideology invoking biology in the form of genes and hormones to explain gender-segregated human behavior. We will come back to this issue.

What was Horney's substitute for Freud's biologism? What was Horney's ultimate beginning? Although she acknowledged biology, she believed that it was *culture* that had the correct answers about the shapes of our souls. As if parodying the saying, "*to biology we owe our life, to culture our humanity,*" Horney turned to a new beginning in psychoanalytic theory that emphasized the indelible imprint of human relationships on human character. From a psychoanalytic viewpoint, it is easy to see how Freud's theory was gender-driven in some of its main characteristics: the Darwinian survival of the fittest (clearly the male), the triumph of competitive individualism as an ideology, and the imperialism of a theory that wanted to supersede anthropology in its widest sense.

These characteristics of the theory become more glaring when compared with Karen Horney's own theoretical parameters. Horney was the first woman to openly rebel and break with the Freudian establishment. Her theory, although also having the clear imprint of a woman, went philosophically quite beyond gender determination. In contrast to a theory of the ego that more and more emphasized the accumulation model of capitalism (as reflected in so-called deficit theories), her theory postulated a *self*, the resultant of modes of connectedness contingent on social context.

Etymologically culture means breeding, cultivation, nourishment. It definitely has a feminine connotation. It means aliment, development, growth, and context (container). That is exactly what we are talking about: connections, relationships. Horney placed the emphasis of psychoanalytic psychology on the necessary relativity of human behavior to its context, to its connections, as shown by the fact that her theory of the development of neurosis is based on interpersonal strategies that become internalized and compulsive.

In this regard it is important to examine the attitude of Freud and of Horney toward the sciences of context, of culture, such as anthropology, ethnology, sociology. As we all know, Freud was a systemic thinker like Marx and Darwin. He was also quite ambitious at that. Freud's project was to create a psychoanalytic anthropology in the widest sense of the word. The explanatory power of psychoanalysis would thus extend to embrace all the human sciences, and ultimately supersede them. I have called this sort of cannibalistic attitude scientific imperialism.

Here Horney presents us with another interesting contrast. She had an explicit attitude that is also opposite to Freud's, which is reflected throughout her writings: We ought to make connections with anthropology, sociology, ethnography, and related sciences. This, she said, is necessary in order to help each other understand the complexity of the matter at hand, the human being, which is the object of so many sciences.

As a man who possessed the unconditional regard of his mother, Freud probably felt more entitled and ambitious. He was a conqueror, a Moses. Typically Horney, who had a distant and absent father, had to struggle through monumental obstacles to attain the stature she achieved. However, Horney's mother did help—by traditional patriarchal standards—in her odd development.

Thus we see how gender is reflected in the opus and biography of these psychoanalytic theoreticians, necessarily determining much of their direction. Freud's earlier women disciples were by and large dutiful daughters. They did contribute no doubt, at times in surreptitious ways. We cannot deny the contributions of Helene Deutsch, Marie Bonaparte, and Melanie Klein. The latter took up the thread of "connections" in Freud's theory, the "object" part of the instinct theory, what the instinct connects to. Melanie Klein created an epistemologically fascinating theory of "object relations" that also follows the feminine pattern I am talking about. However, perhaps because of oedipal guilt and in a counterphobic manner, she titrated her theory with ultrainstinctivism: "The infant projects the death instinct on the mother's breast," for example.

As it has been stated so many times, it is the merit of Horney to have been the first to openly rebel and break with dogmatic Freudianism. This was by no means easy, and if we carefully read her early writings, we can see the struggle reflected. As already pointed out by Alexandra Symonds, it is also to Horney's merit to have gone beyond gender determinism to give us a gender-free theory, a theory that applies equally to all humans. To remain gender-driven is to identify with the aggressor. This helps the aggressor because it keeps us divided.

Let me turn now to clinical observations that I made in the course of my career as a child psychiatrist. I have done much work with adolescents, and there are three memorable facts that are not much discussed in the psychiatric literature, which are relevant to this discussion.

1. For children, the rates of prevalence of mental disorders by and large are loaded toward males. In other words, if you look at the literature on epidemiology of childhood mental disorders, you will see that most of them are 2 to 10 times more frequent in young boys. An inversion takes place in adolescence, a time when mental illness becomes more prevalent in teenage girls. Most explanations of this phenomenon tend to focus on hormonal changes and imbalances. However, this phenomenon is isomorphic with Gilligan's and others' discoveries of what happens to the self of women at this age.

2. Although the number one diagnosis for inpatient adolescent boys is conduct disorder, the equivalent for girls is depression. This means that males at this age strike out, while females turn against themselves. Of course, many of these boys end up in correctional facilities rather than hospitals, and that is one of the reasons for the differential in prevalence; however, it also indicates a different societal attitude toward boys' and girls' deviant behavior, with a tendency for the latter's behavior to be more invalidated. The boys' behavior, although still deviant, is not annulled by a psychiatric diagnosis. To put it differently, the boys' deviance or rebellion is ultimately more recognized as a free act of will.

3. The available data about victims of child abuse, in all its forms, reveals something along the same lines: Males who were abused as children tend to identify with the aggressor. As adults, they will predominantly be victimizers. Women, on the other hand, identify with the victim. As adults, they will be victims of abuse, whether it is rape, the battered wife syndrome, or all the other possible physical and emotional forms of abuse.

Let me submit to you that Freud did stumble upon a clinical observation, which led to a shy theoretical lead, that could have brought him to a more humanistic, although not biologistic psychoanalytic construct. This is the *seduction theory.* As you know, this was a brief theoretical interlude in Freud's career, which he gave up when he discerned that some patients only had seduction fantasies. This matter has been the subject of much discussion lately and already Kohut acknowledged that, after a detour of many years, he returned to the seduction theory. It is Horney, however, who developed a seduction theory, although not expressly acknowledged as such. Kohut developed many of Horney's ideas, the self theory included, but he gave her no credit at all.

It is most pertinent to talk about a theory of seduction today, since this is an affair that has been traditionally portrayed to occur between the sexes, a gender affair, so to say. It seems that some of Freud's patients had truly been sexually abused as children, but he discarded their stories in favor of the fantasy theory that ultimately led to the Oedipus complex. Freud's mistake was not to have taken seduction in its symbolic sense. Had he done that, he would have realized that all his patients had in fact been symbolically seduced. Let me explain.

If you enter into a relationship with someone who is much weaker than you and who desperately needs you for dire survival, you may have and, in fact, often have the power to shape this person's behavior to fit your own needs. You can be sexually exploitative or you can exploit this person's work and resources for your own benefit. You can also be psychologically and emotionally exploitative, thus subduing your "object" and shaping his or her subjectivity. This seduction is perhaps the less obvious, but no doubt the more insidious. Hence we have to turn the tables on seduction and see it for what it really is from this new perspective, a power issue. It is the issue of the slave subdued by the master that Hegel talked about.

How is Horney's work a theory of seduction? She tells us that in order to feel safe, to feel like she or he belongs, the child has to develop strategies that please the parent. It is these strategies that later shape the neurotic character, but they are ultimately developed in response to the parents' power, in order to obtain their acceptance, their recognition. This is how parents may seduce the child, by shaping the child's character and depriving the child of his or her natural course—seducing his or her soul.

I started this paper by talking about the Church's Council, with its agenda on gender and soul. Let's ask ourselves today: What is the standard for measuring our souls today? What is the standard for humanity? How do you measure humanity? Here again, Freud and Horney offered opposite answers. For the former, the utopia of human fulfillment is genitality, defined as sexual functioning and enjoying in a social context of monogamy, heterosexuality, and other prevailing social values such as gender difference. Therefore, the standard for measuring humanity is external to the individual.

The ego psychology school, after Freud, went even further in emphasizing ego strength, as I said, after the accumulation model of capitalism. Of course, the ultimate model of ego strength is not a woman, a child, an elderly person, or a so-called minority person. I am afraid the ultimate model of humanity here is a white, Anglo-Saxon, wealthy, and politically powerful male, as Igor Caruso already pointed out quite a few years ago. In fact, I was asked to contribute this paper, because, like women, I am not fully recognized by those standards.

Horney's answer to the same question, the question of the standard to measure humanity, is quite different. Here again, she stresses a relationship, a connection, in this case the connection to ourselves. The standard of humanity is thus internal for the individual. It consists in the congruence between being and its concept or image, the match between what I am and what I think I am, what I also demand others to recognize me for. It is in reaching my real self that I attain full humanity. The health of the soul is based on freedom from distortion of our own value. Our self-assessment impacts on how we know the world at large, in our reality testing. Corollary is free activity, the activity that I effect to build my self over the ruins of what they made of me, and in the context of my project for myself. "Know thyself" is an old adage, but it had never been spelled out in this depth.

REFERENCE

Horney, K. (1967/1973). *Feminine Psychology,* H. Kelman et al. (Eds.). New York: Norton.

EPILOGUE

MILTON M. BERGER, M.D.

In the introduction to this book and in the contributions that follow it, there is more than sufficient data to refute the "anatomy is destiny" belief of Freud and his followers. Unfortunately, this belief is maintained to this day to the detriment of girls and women who are still treated in all too many families, groups, and cultures in our country and abroad as if they were inferior.

This book of proceedings of the historic November 2, 1991, conference entitled *Women Beyond Freud: New Concepts of Feminine Psychology* is another milestone in the struggle of women to become first-class citizens in all cultures. The ongoing battle to bring enlightenment about females also brings positive changes in the long-held beliefs about, and burdens inflicted on, males because of their genetically determined gender. The goals of increased enlightenment and unshackling of the chains that still bind males and females will be served if we move toward changed attitudes and behaviors between males and females through the new understanding brought to us by our authors.

Karen Horney gave the psychoanalytic world an indication of what was forthcoming from her when, at age 37, she presented her paper "On the Genesis of the Castration Complex in Women" at the 1922 Seventh International Psychoanalytical Congress in Berlin, where Freud was serving as chairman. Gay, in his biography of Freud, states: "By the early 1920s Freud seemed to have adopted the position that the little girl is a failed boy, the grown woman is a kind of castrated man." Horney was also responding in her paper to Abraham's article (1921) "Manifestations of the Female Castration Complex," which elaborated on and agreed with Freud's postulations. Horney suggested a revised version of penis envy. She did not deny its existence but placed it within a context of normal female development. "Penis envy does not create femininity" Horney said, "but rather expresses it." Hence she rejected the idea that this envy necessarily leads women to the repudiation of their womanhood. Quite to the contrary, "We can see that penis envy by no means precludes a deep and wholly womanly love attachment to the father." Horney was, from the Freudian perspective that dominated these congresses, behaving in the most correct manner possible: she respectfully cited the founder; she accepted the very idea of penis envy. She only speculated, a little dryly: perhaps it was "masculine narcissism" that had led psychoanalysts to accept the view that woman, after all half the human race, is discontented with the sex that nature has assigned to her. It seemed as though male analysts found this view "too self-evident to need explanation." Whatever the reasons, the conclusion psychoanalysts had drawn about woman, Horney argued "is decidedly unsatisfying, not only to feminine narcissism but also to biological science."

The contributions presented herein give clear unrefutable evidence that the emotional, psychological, sociological, religious, economic, and political beliefs and practices of each cultural group, small as well as large, are responsible for the attitudes toward and the status of women. Data and documentation that allow for increased respect for the personhood of females as well as males while undermining the objectification of both sexes open a major pathway toward the humanization of men, women, and children throughout the world.

REFERENCES

Abraham, K. (1921). Manifestations of the female castration complex. *International Journal of Psycho-analysis*, 3, 1.

Gay, P. (1988). *Freud: A Life for Our Time*. New York: Norton.

Horney, K. (1924). On the genesis of the castration complex in women. *International Journal of Psycho-analysis*, 5, 50–65.